SEA OF JAPAN

KOREA

JAPAN

Tokyo

Osaka KANAGAWA
Prefecture

PACIFIC OCEAN

The Gateway To Japan

KANAGAWA

The official seal of Kanagawa Prefecture

CONTENTS

GREETINGS

Fifteen years ago, that is, in January, 1946, I had the pleasure of assuming office here in Yokohama as the Governor of Kanagawa Prefecture. At that time, however, the cities of Yokohama and Kawasaki had been reduced to ashes, while industries of this Prefecture were in a state of almost total destruction.

Agriculture alone survived the war devastation. But what little foodstuff produced by agriculture in Kanagawa Prefecture was hardly sufficient to feed even one-third of the population of this prefecture at that time.

Furthermore, airplanes of the U. S. Occupation Forces used to take off and land in the central section of Yokohama City. And the flag, Stars and Stripes, was flying from all the buildings that had survived fire in this city. Conditions in those days could perhaps properly be described as if the entire Kanagawa Prefecture was under the occupation of the Allied Forces.

My first thought upon the assumption of my duties as the Governor of Kanagawa Prefecture was to direct what little I could still accomplish toward the rehabilitation of our mother country. And I stepped up my efforts toward that goal by encouraging the people of this Prefecture.

My road ahead, nevertheless, was hazardous; it was replete with difficulties on all sides.

Now, Kanagawa Prefecture has never been favored with rich natural resources; the entire Prefecture was virtually at the extreme of privation and hardship; and the general public were experiencing immense difficulties just to maintain sheer sustenance.

But we worked hard together -- the people of Kanagawa Prefecture in general, and those of us in public service; we made undaunted efforts toward the rehabilitation of our mother country, simultaneously offering our sincere cooperation with the Occupation Administration, thus contributing our share toward the establishment of a strong foundation on the basis of which the San Francisco Peace Treaty could be brought forth.

Coveted independence was regained in 1952; Japan was once again permitted to return to the international society of nations. Furthermore, Japan was elected to membership in the United Nations Organization in 1956 for the fulfillment of our national aspirations.

Incidentally, we are convinced that our strenuous endeavors of promoting a public campaign, aimed at the dissemination and propagation of our ideas as regards the Japanese cooperation with the UN spirit had to some extent accounted for the Japanese regaining of international goodwill and faith.

I am happy to note that our Kanagawa Prefecture has recovered from the severe blow it had suffered in the last war, and that we are making a good headway in every aspect, at a pace that surpasses the prewar level. Particularly noteworthy is our development in manufacturing industries and the re-establishment of wholesome finances; we are next only to Tokyo and Osaka in our progress throughout the nation.

And we are ready to forge ahead still further to make Kanagawa Prefecture a place where one would be happy to live, with everything geared to the international level.

Naturally, we realize that there are yet many things to be accomplished, as we reflect upon the existing conditions of overland traffic, social welfare, the education system and facilities, environment sanitation, the housing situation, and the other items that come under the general heading of administrative problems.

These problems, however, serve only as a source of inspiration to carry still further our efforts to deal with them successfully.

Meanwhile we have herewith compiled a booklet that will help direct one's thoughts backward in time to trace the path that Kanagawa Prefecture has followed in the course of the last 15 years, and also to show the present extent of our achievements during the period under review.

It is our pleasure to present friendly nations abroad with this booklet, with a thought that they might see, through the pages of this booklet, what progress we of Kanagawa Prefecture are making, and by inference, what development Japan as a whole is making. For it is our cherished hope that their knowledge of the present situation in Kanagawa Prefecture and in Japan may contribute to the promotion of better understanding and friendship between them and us of Japan.

Mention might also be made in closing that Kanagawa Prefecture has played host to the U. S. armed forces more than any other prefecture throughout the nation during the postwar years, either in the form of the Occupation Forces or as the U. S. Security Forces stationed in Japan as at present.

There is no denying that their presence in this Prefecture has incurred some burden upon the shoulders of people in Kanagawa Prefecture.

On the other hand, the people of Kanagawa Prefecture have also had the opportunities to learn many things from these Americans, besides having received great stimulation toward industrial rehabilitation. Moreover, we have received constant encouragement, morally and materially, from the Americans in the military service as well as from their family members. And this, we will always remember with sincere gratitude.

I, in my capacity as the Governor of Kanagawa Prefecture, hereby make a special mention of this fact by way of expressing my heartfelt appreciation of what they have generously done for us.

IWATARO UCHIYAMA

Governor, Kanagawa Prefecture

Profile of Kanagawa Prefecture

The cities of Tokyo and Yokohama are widely known internationally. Adjoining the capital city of Tokyo, and embracing the international port city of Yokohama, is Kanagawa Prefecture.

Kanagawa Prefecture is situated approximately in the central part of Japan's Main Island. Its circumscribed area is 2,361 square kilometers, which is the forth smallest in the national ranking; in population, however, it ranks 7th with 3,440,000 (1960) in the national standings. The density is 1,458 persons per square kilometer, which is next only to Tokyo and Osaka, or third.

Kanagawa's population shows a steady increase annually. In recent years, the rate of growth is approximately 100,000 persons a year.

There are all told 14 cities, 24 towns and one village within Kanagawa Prefecture, including such large cities as Yokohama and Kawasaki. And more than 90 percent of the total population within this Prefecture are resident in the city areas, leading to annual inflation of the urban population.

The topography of Kanagawa Prefecture may be roughly classified into the mountainous area of the west, the plains area of the east, and the maritime area of the south.

The cities of Yokohama and Kawasaki are situated in the eastern flat area.

Yokohama has continued developing as an international port city since its opening to foreign trade in 1858; it has also functioned as Japan's "front door" throughout. At present, this city is inhabited by 1,380,000 persons, and occupies an important position as the central city of this Prefecture.

Foreign trade through Yokohama was temporarily affected severely, what with World War II and the postwar occupation by the Allied Forces. Today, however, it has recovered to the extent of surpassing the prewar level; the combined total of exports and imports in 1959 amounted to ¥517,400 million in value, which represented 20 percent of the national total.

Kawasaki, on the other hand, is a representative industrial city of Japan. Together with the adjoining maritime industrial zone of Yokohama, Kawasaki constitute the central part of the Tokyo-Yokohama Heavy Industry Belt

which is one of the most thriving industrial centers of Japan. There are many large factories of basic industries concentrated here.

The enormous productivity of this area comprises a major pillar supporting Japan's economic growth.

Incidentally, Kanagawa Prefecture's industrial production centered around the Kawasaki area amounted to ¥1,000,000 million in value, or approximately 10 percent of the aggregate national total in 1959.

Of the total working populace of 1,560,000 persons in Kanagawa Prefecture, 42.7 percent of them are absorbed in these manufacturing industrial enterprises.

Manufacturing industries are thus the most prominent single factor in all the industrial activities of this Prefecture, playing the role of the prime mover in the general development of Kanagawa Prefecture.

Down toward the south in the eastern plains area is Yokosuka. This port city serves as the base of operation for the U.S. Navy of the U.S. Security Forces stationed in Japan, constituting a strategic point in Japan's national defense.

There is the port of Misaki on Miura Peninsula; this port is nationally famous as the base of operation for Japan's deep sea fishing industry. The tuna catch landed here correspond to 57 percent of the national total.

There is a string of cities, such as Kamakura, Fujisawa, Chigasaki, Hiratsuka and Odawara along the maritime area in the southern part of this Prefecture.

The climate here is mild throughout the four seasons of the year, and the area is favored with natural scenic beauty. This area in general has been known since olden times as a suitable place for recreation and health resorts. It is also endowed with excellent sites for surf bathing.

Together with Kyoto and Nara, Kamakura is one of the oldest cities of Japan; places of historical interests as well as objects of valuable cultural heritage are preserved in abundance.

In the western mountainous area, there are Mt. Hakone and the Tanzawayama mountain group.

Hakone is noted for scenic beauty and many hot springs; this area is designated as one of the National Parks of Japan.

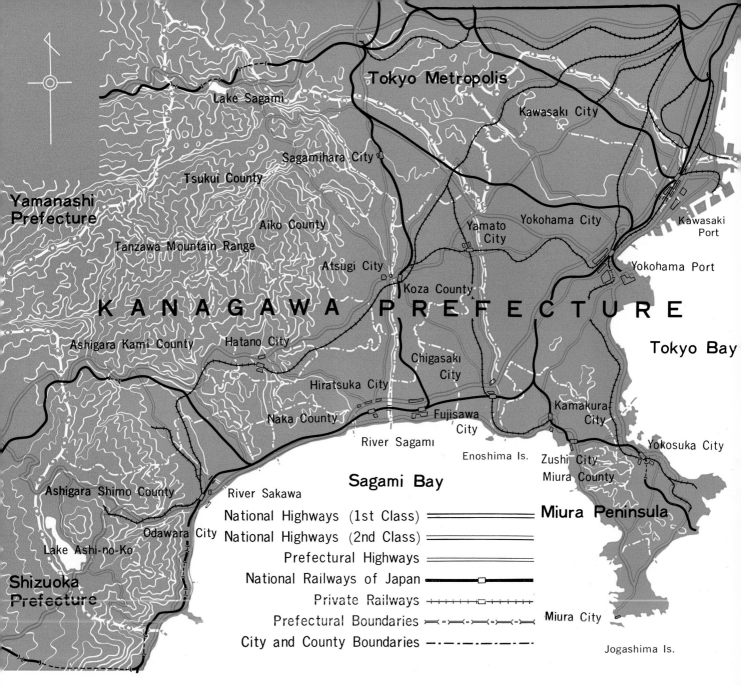

National Highways (1st Class) ══════════
National Highways (2nd Class) ══════════
Prefectural Highways ══════════
National Railways of Japan ━━━━□━━━━
Private Railways ┼┼┼┼┼□┼┼┼┼┼
Prefectural Boundaries ━‹‹›‹‹›‹‹›‹‹›‹━
City and County Boundaries ━·━·━·━·━

Map of Kanagawa Prefecture

Hakone used to be a natural barrier along the Tokaido route connecting the west with the east in Japan, offering immense difficulties in traffic and communications. Today, however, paved highways run in all directions, throughout the mountainous area of Hakone, affording pleasant drives.

The central part of Kanagawa Prefecture constitutes the agrarian area. Agriculture in this Prefecture has features that characterize the enterprises in the area adjoining large cities—that is, the cultivation of vegetables and fruits, and livestock raising occupy a prominent proportion in the total agricultural activities.

In recent years, however, industrial development pro-jects are cutting inroads into the hinterland areas; as a result, a new industrial zone is in the making in the hinter-land area.

A large population within a limited area; major indus-trial areas connected with international trade ports; pic-turesque scenery and rich cultural heritage—such are the characteristic features of Kanagawa Prefecture, symboliz-ing the thriving new Japan, in contrast to the Japan of old, quaint traditions!

In this sense, Kanagawa Prefecture might well be called a representative "face" of Japan today, embodying her aspirations and national strength, as well as her high hopes and inner difficulties.

Toward
a Life of Abundance
and Peace

15 Years After the War,
Having recovered completely from the war devastation,
In all the aspects of economic, social and cultural activities,
Japan is making a new development that surpasses the prewar level
— and
We, the people of Kanagawa Prefecture,
In our search for
The land of peace and abundance, and
A life in peace and abundance,
Keep forging ahead incessantly!

pectacular
Economic
Growth

Keihin Heavy Industry Zone

Industry

Japan's industrial production has shown a remarkable increase during the past ten years, so much so that the 1960 index, on the basis of 100 for 1951, amounted to 377 or almost four times as much. The progress has thus been the prime power source supporting the high level of economic growth of the nation.

Kanagawa is one of the most prominent industrial prefectures in Japan; the growth of industrial production in 1960, too, reached 669 in terms of the index of 100 for 1951; the figure is definitely larger than the national average. The value of industrial production amounted to $2,779 million which represents approximately ten percent of the national total.

As of the end of 1960, there were 6,919 factories within Kanagawa Prefecture, having 443,000 persons on their payrolls. Manufacturing industries absorbed 35 percent of the total number of persons engaged in some kind of productive activities, earning approximately 41 percent of the total individual income for the Prefecture. Furthermore, these percentages show a tendency to become higher annually.

Particularly worthy of note is the fact that the maritime industrial zone of Yokohama and Kawasaki is one of the four major industrial centers of the nation; there are concentrated here a large number of heavy and chemical enterprises equipped with highly efficient productive facilities of the latest type.

And, their enormous productive activities contribute substantially toward the national progress of industrial growth as a whole.

It will be recalled that the industrial activities in Kanagawa Prefecture (which embraces the productive center of the Keihin or Tokyo-Yohohama area) were reduced to a state of almost total devastation in 1946—or in the wake of World War II. Five years later, the production still remained at about one-half of the prewar level.

The outbreak of hostilities in Korea, and the subsequent all round business recovery throughout the world, encouraged the revival of iron and steel making as well as the machinery manufacturing industry in Kanagawa Prefecture.

Along with the larger exports, promotion of greater

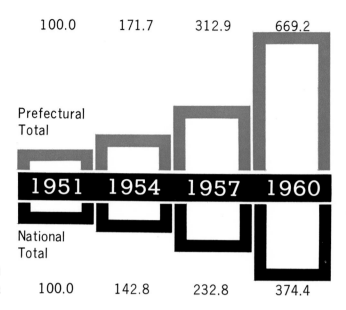

| 100.0 | 171.7 | 312.9 | 669.2 |

Prefectural
Total

| 1951 | 1954 | 1957 | 1960 |

National
Total

Expansion of Industrial Production
— Industrial Production Index

| 100.0 | 142.8 | 232.8 | 374.4 |

equipment investments, and the substantial increase in domestic consumption, there was a steady build-up of Kanagawa's productive activities; the tempo of growth was further accelerated in and after 1955, on the strength of new stimuli furnished in the form of a technical revolution.

During the ten year period from 1951 to 1960, the output of machinery increased ten times; chemical products, 4.6 times; iron and steel, 3.6 times; foodstuffs, 3.2 times; and fibers (textiles), 2 times. This productive expansion was impressive.

As the scope of productive activities became further enlarged, so the demand for land as industrial sites has also become intensified; the number of enterprises which sought their base of operation in Kanagawa Prefecture which maintains the major consumption market of the Tokyo-Yokohama area also recorded a sudden increase.

It has thus become a matter of urgent necessity to create new industrial zones. In and after 1947, therefore, land reclamation work along the seashores facing Tokyo Bay, as well as land development for industrial purposes

in the hinterland, has been pushed vigorously in Kanagawa Prefecture.

It is true that individual enterprises have devoted much effort toward the technical improvement of their industrial activities. Meanwhile, however, the Kanagawa Prefectural Government has also realized its plans of having better means of experiment and research, as evidenced by the establishment of the Industrial Experiment Station, the Industrial Handicraft Guidance Agency and the like. For the purpose of public enlightenment on better industrial techniques, special courses were organized and demonstrations given, thereby facilitating the wider practice of advanced production methods.

As a measure of assisting further modernization of industrial equipment, moreover, the Prefectural Government has created a system of advancing loans to various major industrial enterprises. This practice has also proved a big stimulation for minor enterprises to install new and better mechanical equipment with their private funds. Higher efficiency and productivity have thus been promoted.

Iron and Steel

There has been a remarkable increase in iron and steel production in Kanagawa Prefecture in recent years, in sequence to the general rise in demand and also to the phenomenal expansion of the productive equipment.

Steel ingot production in 1960 amounted to 2 million tons. Meanwhile the total production of metals, including non-ferrous metals, amounted to 6,750,000 tons.

There are such iron foundries as the Kawasaki, Tsurumi and Mizue Works of Nippon Kokan, and the Kawasaki works of Fuji Iron and Steel Co. where an integral process from the pig iron to steel is carried out. These, together with approximately 160 other plants, in conjunction with still other related enterprises, constitute the nucleus of the heavy industry enterprises in this prefecture.

Shipbuilding

Shipbuilding has been a major industry in Kanagawa Prefecture since olden times. There are at present 59 shipyards where wooden and steel ships of 500 tons and larger can be built.

Shipbuilding as an enterprise has suffered waves of bad times on a number of occasions after the last war. Thanks to the series of Planned Shipbuilding Programs and the ship export boom, however, the new steel ships built in 1960 totaled 161 vessels, 295,000 tons; meanwhile 3,736 ships were repaired.

The largest shipbuilding berth operated within Kanagawa Prefecture is capable of building a 50,000 ton ship: there are eight shipbuilding berths of 10,000 tons and upward in capacity; the largest dock is of 26,000 tons, and there are two 10,000 ton docks in addition.

In view of the recent trend of building larger ships, efforts are also being made to enlarge the capacity of existing shipbuilding berths.

Automobiles

Kanagawa Prefecture has become the largest automobile producing prefecture in Japan, having three major automobile manufacturing companies of this nation operating their main factories within this prefecture.

In 1960, the total production amounted to 140,000 units, including 28,000 passenger cars, 94,000 chassis for trucks, 3-wheel trucks, and buses.

Electric Machinery

The manufacture of electric machinery, together with the production of the means of conveyance, constitute one of the greatest of all the industrial activities within Kanagawa Prefecture. Especially since 1955, the industry has shown rapid growth by four times along with an unusual progress of home electrification.

Both in the field of light and heavy electric machinery manufacturing, there are a number of enterprises where they employ more than 5,000 workers; almost all the top companies of Japan are operating in this prefecture.

The products cover an extensive variety, from transistor radio receiving sets to huge generators, as well as such "flowers" of modern times as electronic calculating machines and missiles. The export of radio receiving sets is also remarkably active.

Petroleum Refining

A visitor to the maritime area of Kawasaki and Tsurumi will find tremendous facilities for petroleum refining and storage towering along the coast. More of such facilities are to be erected in this neighbourhood when the land reclamation work now going on shows further progress.

It is scheduled that the petroleum refining capacity in this area will reach 43,000 kiloliters per month, and the storage capacity, 700,000 kiloliters.

Petrochemical Industry

Japan's petrochemical industry has made a phenomenal development in recent years. And a huge combination of the petrochemical enterprises with the petroleum refining industry, the largest in scale in Japan, has been established in the maritime industrial zone of Kawasaki. Meanwhile plans are under way to promote such a petrochemical "kombinat" in Yokohama and Yokosuka as well.

23

● Chemical Industries

The production of fertilizer, electrolytic soda, dye stuffs, synthetic resin, synthetic fibers and films constitute the nucleus of the chemical industry activities in Kanagawa Prefecture.

There are more than 200 factories engaged in such chemical enterprises. Their combined total production in 1960 was valued at ¥111,200 million which is next only to foodstuff production, and ranked 4th in prefectural standings.

Photo film production

Chemical seasoning in preparation

● Foodstuff

The year 1868 witnessed the production of the first Japanese brewed beer, to blaze the path for modern foodstuff manufacturing industries. And, in Kanagawa Prefecture, foodstuff production is today a major industrial enterprise, side by side with iron and steel, machinery, and chemical products manufacturing.

The list of manufactures grows steadily, e.g., beer, chemical seasonings, flour, confectionary, refined sugar, condensed milk, canned goods and so forth.

The combined total production of foodstuffs in 1960 amounted to ¥147,100 million in value, to be placed third in the national prefectural ranking.

A thermal power station at Yokosuka

● Electric Power Industry

The electric power consumption in Kanagawa Prefecture amounts to 5,500 million KWH a year, and it is expected to increase to 10,500 million KWH in 1965 in view of the fact that there is the Keihin (Tokyo-Yokohama) heavy industry center located within this Prefecture.

Along the sea coast of Tokyo Bay, there have been two thermal power stations since before the war. More thermal power stations have either been completed or are now under construction here, at such points as Kawasaki, Yokohama and Yokosuka, to be completed in 1963. They will have a combined total power generation capacity of 35,000 million KW upon completion.

● Progress and Popularization of Industrial Techniques

Japan's industrial productivity has shown a spectacular progress in recent years as a result of the remarkable advancement in her industrial methods. And Kanagawa Prefectural Government, in 1949, established the Industrial Experimental Station for the purpose of instigating a wider popularization of such advanced industrial techniques.

This Station is made up of five departments, machinery, inorganic chemistry, organic chemistry, raw materials and fibers; in addition, there are the Radioactive Isotope Research Laboratory and the Kawasaki Branch Station under its jurisdiction. This Station carries out extensive experiments and research, besides functioning as a consultant agency.

A new building to house this Station is under construction to be completed in 1962, and the total floor space will reach 1,270,000 square meters.

Industrial Experiment Station (above) and isotope radiation room

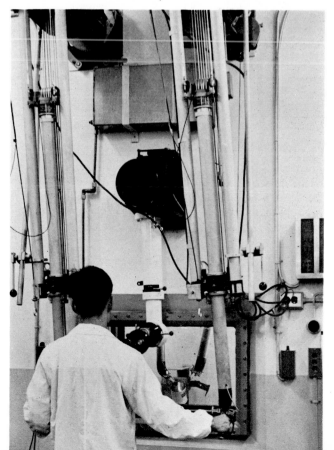

25

Newly created industrial zone in agrarian hinterland

Expanding Industrial Zone

The maritime land reclamation work is making good progress at different places in Kanagawa Prefecture in view of the fact that there has been a hardly saturable demand for new factory sites, along with the steady expansion of industrial activities.

One of these sites is around the river mouth of the Tamagawa which flows along the prefectural border adjoining Tokyo. Kawasaki City completed the reclamation of 92 hectares in 1952. And the Kanagawa Prefectural Government has started the reclamation of adjoining areas extending over 447 hectares, and approximately 80 percent of the work has been accomplished.

It is expected that such major enterprises as petroleum refining, petrochemical enterprises, electric machinery manufacturing and automobile production are to be inaugurated on this newly created factory site.

Land reclamation is also going on along Negishi Bay of Yokohama City, to create 600 hectares of new factory sites before 1967. Here again a large industrial combine of petroleum refining and petrochemical enterprises is to be materialized on the newly created land.

During this time, the industrial zone is making steady inroads into the hinterland areas of Kanagawa Prefecture. In 1960, a total of 245 factories were established, occupying sites totaling 545 hectares. Largest in number among these new factories are those for automobile production, electric and other industrial machinery manufacturing enterprises.

Land reclamation of Kanagawa Pref. Govt. at Kawasaki (photo: Asahi Newspapers)

Handicrafts With Long Tradition

Kanagawa Prefecture is nationally known as a center of a handicraft industry of long history and tradition, in addition to its being a modern industrial hub. The wood works of Odawara and Kamakura are especially famous.

Odawara's wood carving, otherwise known as Hakone souvenirs, has been nationally known since the Heian Period (794–1192). They come in such a wide variety as turned articles, lacquer wares, cabinet work, toys, mosaic and inlaid works; they are hand produced by real experts of many years' training.

Kamakura engravings originated in the Kamakura Period (1193–1392), featuring wood carving and hand finished lacquer ware. Trays of various kind amount to about 30 percent of the products, followed by bowls, boxes and household furniture.

In 1936, the Kanagawa Prefectural Government established the Prefectural Handicraft Center for the purpose of modernization of sundry handicraft industries, with special emphasis attached to the wood carving of the Odawara-Hakone area. In the postwar years, special efforts were made to prevent qualitative deterioration of these handicraft articles, particularly those for export.

Show rooms of Kanagawa Prefectural Handicrafts Guidance Agency

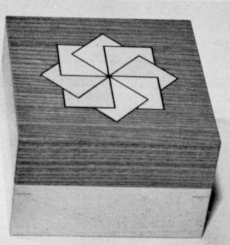

Hakone mosaic work

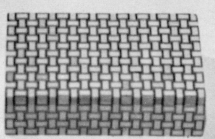

Agriculture

Fluctuation of Agrarian Population

Fiscal Years		Agrarian Population	Agrarian Population / Total Population
1950	National Total	37,810,936	45.4%
	Prefectural Total	565,308	22.7%
1960	National Total	34,545,917	37.0%
	Prefectural Total	462,845	13.4%

Japan's agriculture stands at a major turning point. The national economy has shown a substantial growth with the meteoric development of manufacturing industries at the nucleus after World War II. In the course of such a march of events, however, the difference between the manufacturing industries and agriculture in their productivity and the capacity for earning has been greatly accentuated.

In view of the foregoing development, various measures designed to bring about the modernization of agriculture are being eagerly promoted, so that the difference in the individual income between the cities and agrarian circles will be nullified, and also that agriculture will hold its own in the balanced progress of the national economy.

Agriculture in Kanagawa Prefecture is characterized by a peculiar geographical condition of having the Keihin (Tokyo-Yokohama) industrial zone as well as such large cities as Tokyo and Yokohama close at hand; under the strong influence of such an environment, efforts toward its modernization are also well expedited.

During the years immediately following the war's end, larger production of foodstuffs was the primary concern in the national agricultural activities of Japan. There prevailed in those days an acute shortage of food.

As such a desperate situation was alleviated, agricultural efforts have been directed to more lucrative enterprises, such as the cultivation of vegetables, fruits, livestock raising and so on.

For the last several years, however, the market price of agricultural produce followed a marked tendency to decline, so much so that the smallness of scale in production has come to be affected severely all round.

On the other hand, the rapid development of productive activities in the industrial enterprises, notably that of the Keihin district, has resulted in the advent of new factories and the creation of new residential areas in the central part of the agrarian area of Kanagawa Prefecture; the cultivated land has come to be converted into factory sites and residential areas at a remarkable speed; meanwhile the agrarian man power has been absorbed into other industrial enterprises to such an extent that agriculture now suffers from a noticeable shortage of men. To make the situation even more difficult, the gap is widening in the productivity and earning capacity between manufacturing industries and agriculture.

In the face of such a change in the general situation, Kanagawa's agriculture is also adapting itself to the needs of the times, in such a manner as the introduction of new machines and new production techniques of high standard, in order to improve its productivity. It is a necessity, too, since the old methods of small scale production have been rendered out of date.

Frequently seen at different places within Kanagawa Prefecture where the agrarian people now run their enterprises on a modern basis are such innovations as vinyl houses, green houses, orchard management, livestock raising and cooperative operation of such enterprises among a larger numer of farmers. The progress of these cooperative enterprises in Kanagawa Prefecture has attracted much attention of interested circles in other prefectures.

Meanwhile the Prefectural Government of Kanagawa is also facilitating the modernization and higher productivity of agriculture by giving technical aid to farmers for better management and advanced production methods, as well as financial aid.

1959	Agricultural Production	1950
22.0%	Rice	21.9%
11.2%	Wheats	13.3%
5.6%	Potatoes	16.3%
19.0%	Vegetables	14.9%
9.3%	Fruits	6.3%
26.5%	Livestock Products	15.1%
6.4%	others	12.2%
	TOTAL	

1959		1950

Daikon radish (in the background) and cabbage

Cucumber cultivation within a vinyl house

Agricultural Production of Today

Agriculture in Kanagawa Prefecture shows strong indications of features which characterize agriculture in the suburban areas of all large cities, in view of the geographical proximity to such major cities as Tokyo and Yokohama. Livestock raising, orchard management and cultivation of vegetables constitute a large proportion of the agricultural activities in this Prefecture.

Agricultural production in 1958 amounted to ¥21,336 million in value; this total was 33rd in the national ranking, but 6th in vegetable output and 11th in livestock raising.

Such new and advanced methods of cultivation as vinyl houses, construction of tunnels and hothouses are coming into wider use year after year in this Prefecture. In 1960, for instance, the income from horticultural products, such as vegetables, fruits and floriferous plants amounted to ¥7,700 million or 45 percent of the combined total.

Mikan (mandarine oranges) is the mainstay of the orchard products in Kanagawa Prefecture, followed by pears and chestnuts.

Flowers are cultivated in greenhouses, garden-frames and also in the open, the income resulting from such activities amounting to ¥700 million a year. Hothouse cultivation has become especially popular in recent years. In fact, the output as well as the quality of the carnations, roses, and sweet-peas are at the top level in the nation. In open cultivation, lilies come to the top, with approximately 800,000 bulbs exported annually.

The cultivated areas in Kanagawa Prefecture, as of 1960, amounted to 52,079 hectares, inclusive of paddy fields, dry fields and orchards; the number of agrarian households totaled 73,873 of which 20,733 were engaged exclusively in agricultural work; the agrarian population was 462,838.

Pears

Strawberries

Mikan mandarine oranges

Livestock Raising

Livestock raising is one of the enterprises of which the future is regarded as highly promising. Cattle, pigs and chickens are among the principal objects of this industry in Kanagawa Prefecture. The number of farms engaged in livestock raising has decreased, but the number of animals kept at each of these remaining farms has increased. In chicken raising, for example, there is a marked tendency to keep a larger number to the extent of specializing in this business.

Generally speaking, the scale of livestock raising has become larger, and more of such enterprises are being operated under the cooperative system in recent years.

Dairy-farming in Kanagawa Prefecture stands high in the national ranking. The 1959 supply of milk amounted to 82,000 tons to occupy the 4th rank in the national standing.

Number of Principal Items in Livestock Raising

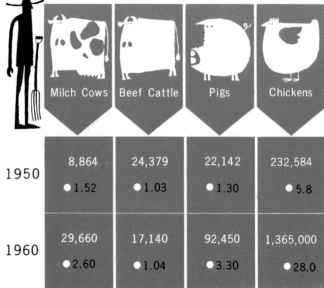

	Milch Cows	Beef Cattle	Pigs	Chickens
1950	8,864 ● 1.52	24,379 ● 1.03	22,142 ● 1.30	232,584 ● 5.8
1960	29,660 ● 2.60	17,140 ● 1.04	92,450 ● 3.30	1,365,000 ● 28.0

Note: ● indicates number per farm

Livestock Breeding Experiment Station

The Livestock Breeding Experiment Station of Kanagawa Prefectural Government undertakes extensive research and experiments on better breeding of domesticated animals and improved management in the livestock industry. In addition, it functions as a consultant agency to give practical advice to interested circles.

Moreover, the Prefectural Government runs a livestock health center at 13 places to give practical services in behalf of livestock farms.

Agricultural Experiment Station

The Agricultural Experiment Station where extensive research is carried out for the modernization of agriculture contributes enormously toward the development of this industry in Kanagawa Prefecture.

Here at this prefectural institution, experiments, research and investigations are conducted not only on the subjects of primary agricultural techniques, such as the betterment of seeds, the improvement of cultivation methods, the study of the qualitative nature of soil and fertilizer, prevention of insect damage and the like, but also on such problems as agricultural management and agrarian livelihood. Furthermore, findings of such intensive studies are disseminated to the agrarian circles through the channels of various organized systems.

The main office of the Agricultural Experiment Station stands in Hiratsuka City but it has a branch station in Odawara where specialized studies are conducted on horticultural enterprises such as the cultivation of vegetables and fruits.

Flower Center

The Flower Center which is tantamount to a botanical garden, which has been under construction for some time in Kamakura City with a budget of ¥140 million, was completed in the early part of 1962.

More than one thousand different species of such flowers as peony, iris, and azalea which were grown at the Prefectural Agricultural Experiment Station over a period of many years constitute the main stay of the collection here.

In addition, all kinds of plants for export and plants in general have been collected, both within and outside of Kanagawa Prefecture, for public exhibition.

The Flower Center aims at cultivation of these flowers as well as promotion of export trade in such garden plants.

Agricultural Modernization in Progress

It is a nationwide trend that modernization is being promoted in agrarian activities, but this is especially the case in Kanagawa Prefecture.

It is true that livestock raising, and cultivation of vegetables and fruits are specially prominent in the agricultural activities of this Prefecture, but an increasing number of these enterprises now specialize in some specific division, instead of all round production.

During this time, positive efforts are being made toward the introduction of agricultural machines of the latest model and trial of intensive cultivation methods, especially in the field of growing vegetables and fruits, utilizing such means as vinyl houses and greenhouses.

Efforts are also being made to run such enterprises on a larger scale through cooperatives, particularly in livestock raising and vegetable cultivation. There are at present 56 instances in which businesses are run on the cooperative system.

In sequence to such attempts at modernization, productivity shows steady improvement. Meanwhile the method of operation, too, shows a tendency to assume the aspect of industrial enterprises of a larger scale, in contrast to that of private farming.

● Land Improvement

In the course of the past 15 years, land improvement has been effected over 28,000 hectares of land, while readjustments (concentration) of cultivated fields have been carried out on an extensive scale, in order to increase the productivity.

Land development enterprises were formerly undertaken primarily for the purpose of increasing the unit output of agricultural produce. Today, however, the work is being promoted under a new guiding principle of preparing the ground for agricultural modernization.

And, along the line of the new concept of agricultural management, concentration of cultivated fields as well as redemarcation of boundries and the widening of agrarian roads are being promoted in a positive manner.

● Agricultural Irrigation

The largest single item in land development enterprises undertaken by the Kanagawa Prefectural Government is the agricultural irrigation project carried out at Sagamihara.

Sagamihara is a plateau area which used to be considered unarable. In order to supply irrigation water to 2,700 hectares of land here, however, the Kanagawa Prefectural Government has built 10 kilometers of water conduits, the first of its kind in Japan. Irrigation to cover the entire district is still under construction.

Upon completion of the irrigation system, the work will account for an additional agricultural production of ¥106 million in value.

Vinyl-house farming

For Higher Productivity

Poultry-farming by a cooperative union

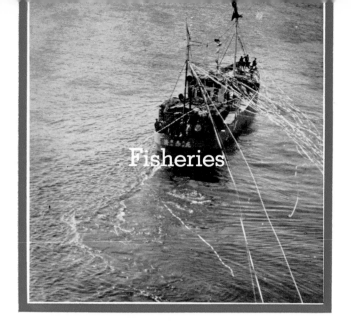

Fisheries

Japan used to be a leading fishing nation of the world. During and after the war years, however, the catch temporarily dropped heavily. Still later, however, the industry recovered rapidly until the yearly catch in 1959 amounted to 5,880,000 tons, thus exceeding the prewar level.

It is to be noted that there has been a specially conspicuous development in deep sea fishing and the near sea fishing in the postwar activities in this field, the combined total of these enterprises amounting to approximately 54 percent of the total catch.

In the case of Kanagawa Prefecture, there is the port of Misaki which is a prosperous base of operation for deep sea fishing. This Prefecture's fishing industry has been dependent largely upon deep sea fishing, and therefore, the effects of war on the industry was specially severe. In 1946—or the year immediately following the war's end—the total catch amounted to only about 24,000 tons.

When deep sea fishing was resumed in full swing, however, the catch has come to show a remarkable increase. In 1958 the prefectural total amounted to 117,000 tons of which 60 percent has been accounted for by deep sea fishing.

Especially conspicuous is the development of tuna and bonito fishing on the high seas. As the type of fishing boats has grown larger, their sphere of activities are now extended even to the Atlantic Ocean.

Besides meeting the domestic demand, part of the deep sea fishing catch is exported to foreign countries in the form of refrigerated maritime products. The industry thus contributes its share to Japan's acquirement of foreign exchange.

As for the coastal fishing, yellow tail fishing, small type trawl fishing and cultivation of sea weed and shell fish constitute the main item of activity. In the near sea fishing, mackerel of various species are the principal catch, and fishermen travel far and wide, going even to Hokkaido and the Japan Sea.

Generally speaking, however, coastal fishing is on the wane. There was the uncontrolled catch immediately after the war; and the land reclamation has been carried out extensively to create new industrial zones; while the source of supply was thus affected, fishing population is too large.

As a basic program to bolster coastal fishing, the Prefectural Government follows the policy of "foster and catch" and has invested a large amount of new capital, notably in the creation of what is referred to as "apartment houses for fish"—the coastal sea bed readjustment —in order to foster the resources of fish supply.

Efforts are also made toward the establishment of better waterfront facilities at fishing ports, headed by that at Misaki where 57 percent of the total amount of tuna catch in Japan is landed. Such fishing port improvement work goes on at 25 ports within the Prefecture.

The improvement of the fishing techniques and the betterment of business management constitute also an important enterprise of the Prefectural Government; it has reinforced the scope and facilities of practical experiments and research of fishing, to disseminate the new learning thus acquired.

The Kanagawa Prefectural Government has also built a number of fishing boats in order to give guidance to deep sea fishing as well as the coastal fishing enterprises. These vessels are engaged in the experiments, research, investigation and cultivation of fishing grounds.

Total Catch Classified According to Division of Fisheries

TOTAL (kg) · 1958		117,230,023
	Horse mackerel	6,188,758
	Mackerel	5,841,621
	Bonito	6,344,689
	Tuna	69,693,379
Total for Fish		101,425,257
Total for Shellfish		11,342,441
Other Maritime Products		2,289,055
Seaweeds		2,173,270

Coastal fishing boats

Deep-sea fishing boats at Misaki Port

● Fishing Port Improvement

Deep sea tuna fishing with Misaki Port as the base of operation is so remarkably active that the catch landed here corresponds to 57 percent of the national total. Tuna fish thus caught are not only distributed throughout the nation but a large portion is exported to the United States and Europe as material for canned food.

The Kanagawa Prefectural Government has shown much interest in the improvement of Misaki Port as a measure of encouragement of deep sea fishing in general.

In 1960, however, a bridge connecting Misaki with Jogashima, a little islet located off the shore of this port, was constructed as part of the program.

Meanwhile land reclamation work is going on along the shores of Jogashima in order to establish facilities for fish processing and cold storage (which go with the deep sea fishing) and also to build a shipyard there.

It was primarily for the effective utilization of these facilities that this bridge has been erected.

Deep Sea Fishing

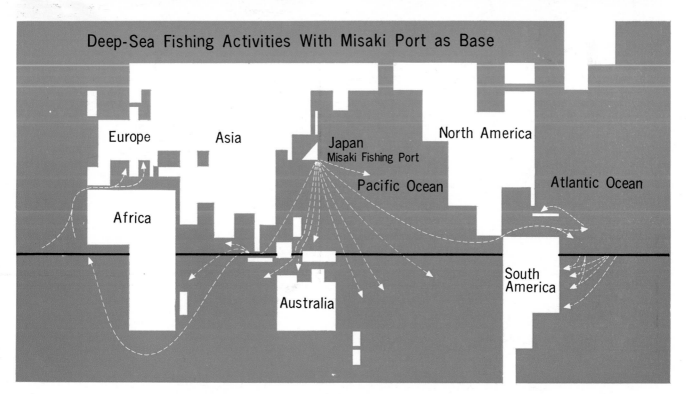

Deep-Sea Fishing Activities With Misaki Port as Base

Europe

Asia

Japan
Misaki Fishing Port

North America

Pacific Ocean

Atlantic Ocean

Africa

Australia

South
America

Apartment Houses for Fish

Positive efforts are being made in Kanagawa Prefecture since 1957 to foster the fishery resources in Sagami Bay. Concrete blocks are dropped into the sea along the shoals in piles in order to cause some change in the direction of undertow of the current, so that it may foster greater growth of plankton and sea weed in the vicinity, to attract more fish.

This enterprise is familiary referred to as the construction of "fish apartment houses" and the work has resulted in a larger catch of such fish as sea bream, flat fish, and mackerel of various species.

Encouragement of Coastal Fishing

Yellow-tail fishing

Nori (sea-weed) being dried in the sun

Successors in Tomorrow's Fisheries

A high school specializing in the three courses of fisheries, maritime products manufacturing and marine engines is operated by the Kanagawa Prefectural Government at Misaki.

Youths graduating from this high school are expected to find their way into the fisheries, merchant shipping and manufacturing industries in general, to develop eventually into technical experts in their respective field of activities, and thus to shoulder Japan's fishing industry of tomorrow.

The Prefectural Government is at present building new school buildings here. Upon their completion, it will become a model fisheries high school.

Foreign Trade

Development of Foreign Trade

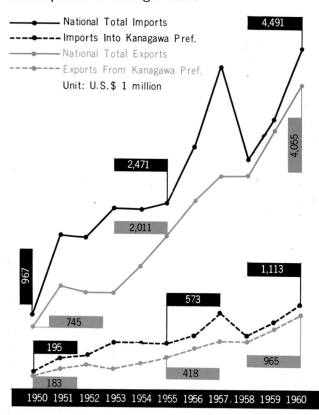

- ●——— National Total Imports
- ●----- Imports Into Kanagawa Pref.
- ●——— National Total Exports
- ●----- Exports From Kanagawa Pref.

Unit: U.S.$ 1 million

4,491

2,471

2,011

967

4,055

1,113

573

745

195

965

183

418

1950 1951 1952 1953 1954 1955 1956 1957 1958 1959 1960

The promotion of more extensive foreign trade is of special importance for Japanese economic growth as well as for the betterment of the national livelihood, in view of the fact that Japan is not favored with much of any natural resources.

In Japan, therefore, government and business together have always exercised immense efforts toward the improvement of trade, particularly exports, through such measures as: the establishment of systems for financing export trade; market research abroad and dissemination of publicity information for Japanese industrial manufactures; structural and constitutional improvement of individual enterprises in order to foster ability to meet commercial competition in the international markets.

Japan's foreign trade was temporarily suspended during the war years. Private international trade was resumed in 1949 to show a steady improvement thereafter.

On the strength of the remarkable rehabilitation of the nation's industrial activities, exports in 1960 amounted to $4,055 million against $4,492 million for imports, the total representing an increase over the prewar level.

Foreign trade through Yokohama, which has always been one of the most active ports of international trade, was slow to recover in the postwar years, however.

For one thing, the major part of the port facilities was placed under the control of the Occupation Forces immediately after the last war. Furthermore, such articles of trade as raw silk and silk goods, which were the flowers of Japan's foreign trade before the war, were relegated to secondary importance after the war, due to a substantial change in the worldwide market situation.

Later, however, general trade through Yokohama has revived rapidly, so much so that the combined total of exports and imports in 1960 amounted to $1,784 million, which represented more than 20 percent of the aggregate national total for that year. Yokohama has once again come to function as a major trade port of this nation.

There are approximately 900 factories within Kanagawa Prefecture which are engaged in industrial production for export; and more than 80 percent of them produce such capital goods as machinery, shipping, metals and chemical products.

Naturally the Kanagawa Prefectural Government has also been active in its efforts of promoting foreign trade. It has participated in various international fairs in order to promote exports; it has dispatched market researchers abroad, along with the efforts toward promoting publicity of Japanese industrial manufactures; it has granted subsidies for the trial manufacture of export products; and it has also granted additional subsidies to the State institutions for financing exports.

What deserves special mention among such efforts for better trade is the establishment of the Silk Center (the International Trade Hall) in the vicinity of Yokohama's waterfront, primarily for the purpose of offering good offices in facilitating exports and also for better international publicity of Japanese industrial manufacturers.

Crude Oil import by a tanker

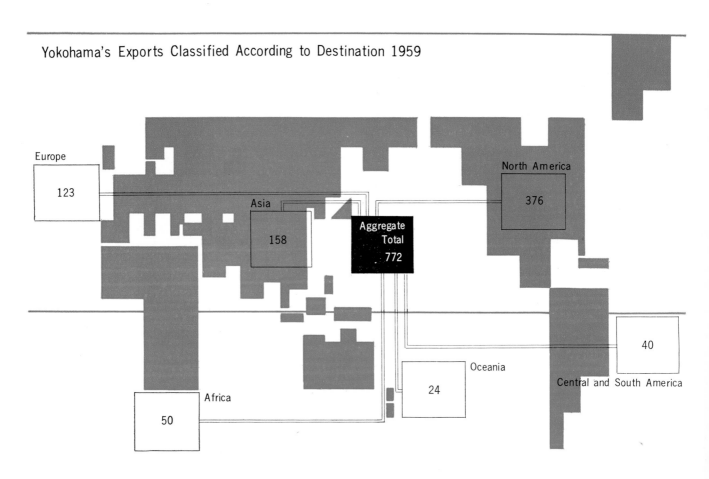

Yokohama's Exports Classified According to Destination 1959

Europe
123

North America
376

Asia
158

Aggregate
Total
772

Africa
50

Oceania
24

Central and South America
40

Unit: U.S. $ 1 million

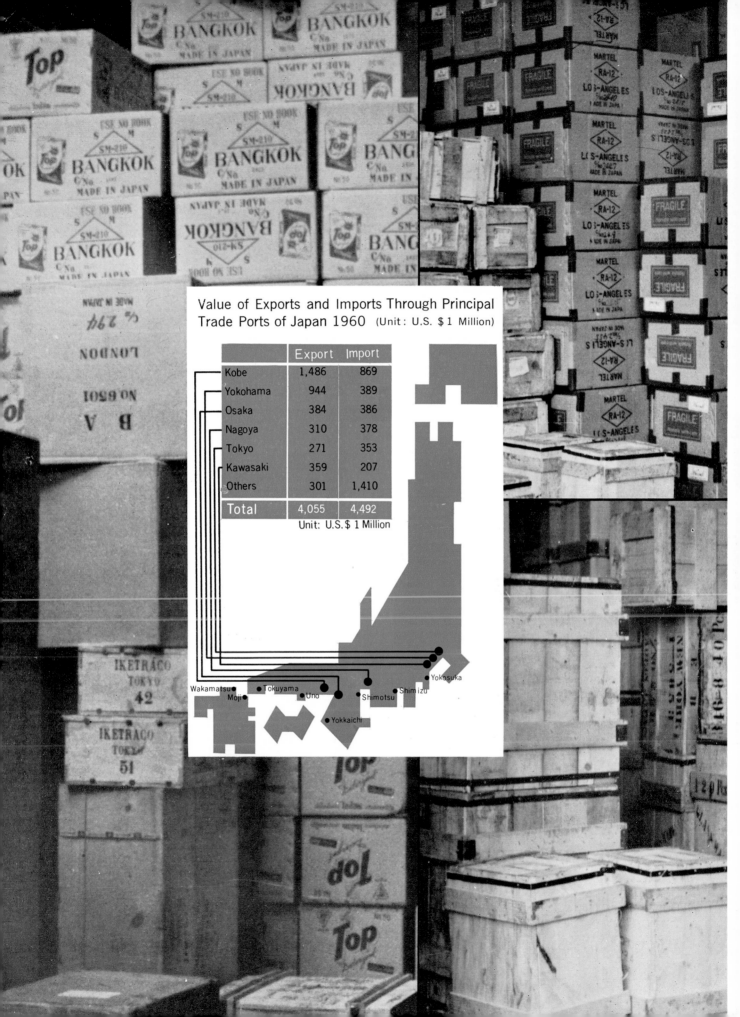

Value of Exports and Imports Through Principal Trade Ports of Japan 1960 (Unit: U.S. $1 Million)

	Export	Import
Kobe	1,486	869
Yokohama	944	389
Osaka	384	386
Nagoya	310	378
Tokyo	271	353
Kawasaki	359	207
Others	301	1,410
Total	4,055	4,492

Unit: U.S. $1 Million

Wakamatsu Moji Tokuyama Uno Yokkaichi Shimotsu Shimizu Yokosuka

Raw Silk

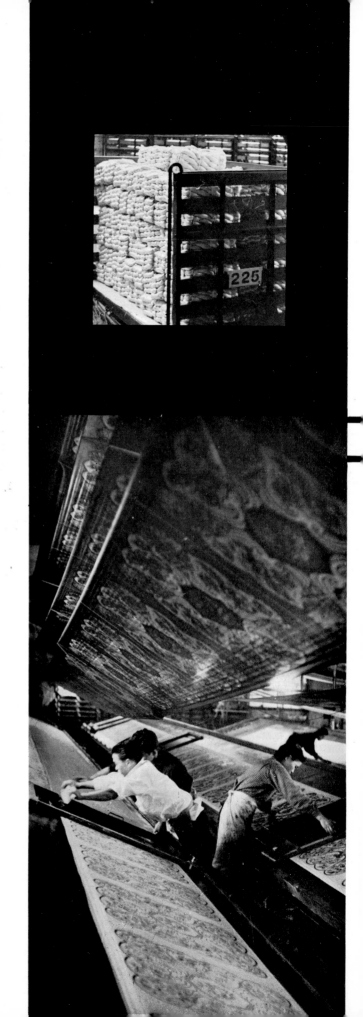

Raw silk is a special product of Japan, and the nation has always been proud of this material; its luster and pleasant touch are simply peerless, and raw silk continues to hold sway over all the fibers of the world.

Raw silk used to be the unrivaled article of Japan's export trade before the war. At one time, 34,857,000 kilograms of raw silk were exported to various countries abroad. And 74 percent of this total was shipped from Yokohama. Raw silk, therefore, was the important item of Yokohama's export trade.

After many years of suspension of trade during the war years, and especially on account of the appearance of new chemical fibers in the meantime, the trade in raw silk has suffered a severe blow in the wake of the war.

In 1947, for instance, raw silk exports amounted to 1,036,380 kilograms or only 3 percent of the prewar peak.

Later, however, the fine qualities of silk came to be better appreciated abroad, leading to a gradual recovery of the export trade. In 1961, Japanese raw silk exports amounted to 4,206,060 kilograms.

Japan's sericultural circles have naturally taken steps toward facilitating the raw silk export, but the Kanagawa Prefectural Government takes special interest in the encouragement of this trade. For instance, it promoted in 1958 the plan for building the Silk Center-International Trade Hall in Yokohama, acting in concert with various interested circles.

This Trade Hall undertakes extensive enterprises of promoting trade, not only of raw silk but also other articles, giving wider publicity abroad to Japanese industrial products being part of its services.

The Silk Center-International Trade Hall was established in Yokohama in October, 1956 under the joint auspices of the Kanagawa Prefectural and Yokohama City Governments as well as various business and industrial interests, primarily for the purpose of promoting foreign trade and tourism, with particular emphasis laid on silk trade. This Hall has been erected in Yokohama in consideration of the significant role that this port city has played in Japan's international commerce and associations.

Established within this International Trade Hall are the Silk Museum, Exhibition Hall of famous products from all parts of this country (for sale on the spot), Information Center for offering good offices in promoting trade in special products of Japan, and the business offices of various trading houses and so forth.

There is also a hotel attached to this Trade Hall to accommodate an increasing number of foreign visitors.

Silk Center

City Planning in Progress

← *In the vicinity of Yokohama: cultivated land is being converted into residential areas everywhere.*　　　*The central part of Yokohama*

Along with the economic growth, the population of Kanagawa Prefecture has shown a rapid increase. During the recent five years, the population has continued growing at the rate of 100,000 a year. The bulk of these citizens are resident in city areas, leading to an endless expansion of the cities.

In the face of such remarkable development, each city in this Prefecture is carrying out rationalization of thoroughfares and establishment of parks and green zones, on the basis of their respective city planning, in order to bring about an orderly expansion of their cities.

The Kanagawa Prefectural Government assumes the attitude of giving pertinent guidance to these individual city planning projects on the wider vista of taking the whole Prefecture into consideration, besides granting subsidies to facilitate the progress of such enterprises.

Some of the major enterprises concerning the highway construction and the establishment of parks are pushed under the direct management of the Prefectural Government.

As regards parks, there are nine of them created for the recreation of the prefectural citizens, including the Shonan Maritime Park which extends from Kamakura to the Shonan area.

It will be recalled that most of the residential houses in such cities as Yokohama and Kawasaki were lost in fires during the war, resulting in an acute shortage of houses. After the war, however, approximately 500,000 houses have been built. It is said, however, that there is still a shortage of 95,000 houses in view of the fact that the population has increased rapidly, while some of the existing houses had become too old.

The prefectural as well as the municipal authorities have hitherto exercised much effort toward the alleviation of the housing shortage. A new development in this connection is the creation of a new form of residential area in which a number of large apartment houses are concentrated at different localities in a systematic manner. Incidentally, efforts are also made to improve the environment of such apartment house projects.

Readjustment of Thoroughfares

All the cities within Kanagawa Prefecture are promoting projects of thoroughfares readjustment on the basis of their respective city planning, essentially for the purpose of facilitating orderly expansion of the cities concerned.

The widening of highways and streets and planting of roadside trees are also carried out systematically.

Efforts are also being made toward making cities fire-proof.

Cities Continue Expanding

The population within Kanagawa Prefecture continues to grow rapidly annually. In the national census of October, 1960, the prefectural population was 3,440,000. Compared with 2,920,000 of 1955, there was an increase of 520,000 during the five year period under review. The ratio of growth is 18 percent, and it is next only to Tokyo and Osaka or third in the national ranking.

More than one-half of this increase are those who have moved into this Prefecture from elsewhere.

Particularly remarkable is the increase of city population, in view of the fact that more than 90 percent of the increase is absorbed into cities. As a result, cities keep on growing endlessly.

(above) In front of Kawasaki Station where readjustment of thoroughfares is being effected. (below) Improved city streets

Increase of Population

Year	Population
1940	2,188,974
1945	1,865,667
1950	2,487,665
1955	2,919,497
1960	3,443,176

Population Density

Country	Density
Kanagawa Prefecture	1,347
Japan	248
U.S.A.	19
United Kingdom	213
France	81
Australia	1
U.S.S.R.	9

52

Parks

*Various kind of parks—sports parks, children's parks
and parks in general—are being created and improved in
different cities within Kanagawa Prefecture, according to
their respective city planning programs. These parks are
for the beautification of cities but are also for the rest
and recreation of the citizens.*

*It is considered that the creation and improvement of
parks are of special importance for modern cities in consideration of the fact that they have come to be densely
populated while the buildings are becoming higher.*

*Apart from these parks under the management of
individual cities, the Kanagawa Prefectural Government
has established eight prefectural parks in different parts
of this Prefecture, including Shonan Maritime Park, and
Hodogaya Park, on a wider vista of taking the whole
Prefecture into consideration. There are, in addition,
three natural parks such as Mt. Tanzawayama also under
prefectural management.*

*All of these prefectural parks are popular among the
general public.*

53

Housing

Another concentration of apartment houses at Yuri-ga-oka (operated by Japan Housing Corporation: photo, Daily Construction Industry Newspaper)

Changes of Situation Affecting Housing

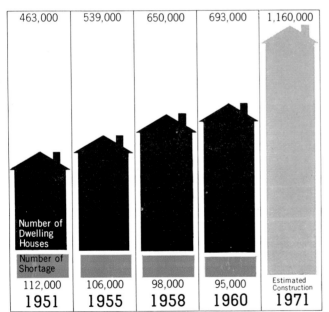

463,000	539,000	650,000	693,000	1,160,000
Number of Dwelling Houses				
Number of Shortage				
112,000	106,000	98,000	95,000	Estimated Construction
1951	**1955**	**1958**	**1960**	**1971**

There prevailed an acute shortage of housing in Kanagawa Prefecture, as elsewhere in Japan, during the years immediately following the war's end. As a measure to alleviate such a difficult situation, strenuous efforts were made to build more houses. In fact, 500,000 dwelling houses were built in this Prefecture up to 1960. Of this total, 15,200 were built under the direct management of the Prefectural Government, while 211,000 of them were built with the aid of other public institutions.

It is said, however, that there still exist a shortage of 95,000 houses in the face of the recent abrupt increase of the population in this Prefecture.

Reflecting such a situation, the creation of new residential areas as well as the construction of new houses are going on at great speed in the suburban areas of large cities and also along the railway lines, such work being pushed both by official institutions as well as by private enterprises.

Particularly noteworthy in recent years is the trend of building large apartment houses, concentrated in large numbers within certain limited areas.

One such enterprise is also promoted by the Kanagawa Prefectural Government in concert with a railway company; the project calls for the construction of 3,600 houses on 494,000 square meters of land at Makigahara of Yokohama City, to be completed some time during 1963.

It is scheduled also that a shopping center, a junior high school, a kindergarten, and children's playground will be built in the vicinity of this new collective residential area as part of the program.

54

The Nation's Capital Zone
For Orderly Expansion

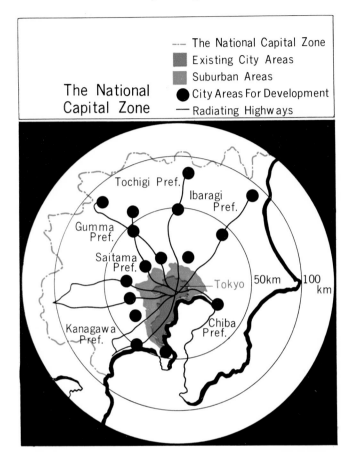

The National Capital Zone

--- The National Capital Zone
■ Existing City Areas
▨ Suburban Areas
● City Areas For Development
— Radiating Highways

The population of the capital city of Tokyo has reached ten million. In sequence to such excessive concentration of the population and business activities, Tokyo is approaching a state of paralysis in many ways.

It is in the face of such a desperate development that an all-embracing program has been worked out to alleviate the situation. with extensive adjoining areas covered in this project of remodelling the capital city.

Wholesale readjustments are to be effected in the means of traffic as well as a general decentralization, notably in the residential areas, thus to create a new national center for Japan's politics, economy and culture, without so much congestion.

The Capital Zone Establishment Law was promulgated in 1955 and the entire circumscribed area of Kanagawa Prefecture has come to be included in this zone.

The capital zone establishment project stipulates, among other things, the restriction of existing cities from becoming enlarged beyond certain prescribed limits, the creation of new satelite cities, and to facilitate the development of these latter cities so that they may absorb surplus population as well as industrial enterprises. It is also stipulated that a "Green Zone" be created between the capital city and satelite cities as suburban areas.

Kanagawa Prefectural Government offers wholehearted support to this program of creating the new capital zone. Four cities of this Prefecture, such as Sagamihara City, have already been designated to function as the said satelite cities.

A concentration of apartment houses at Makigahara (under Prefectural management)

Urgent Need
For
Better
Transportation
Facilities

Highways

Increase in Automobile Traffic Volume per day

Point of Observation	Odawara	Chigasaki	Kawasaki
1948	600	700	1,900
1960	9,100	9,900	21,000

Highway improvement is one of the current as well as pressing problems in Japan in view of the recent spectacular increase in the volume of automobile traffic. And the problem demands an early solution in part for preparation of the ground for further industrial progress.

A survey of recent highway improvement in Kanagawa Prefecture reveals that 52 percent of the highways have been readjusted to accommodate the present volume of traffic; 33.4 per cent have been newly paved; and 96 percent of all the bridges have been reconstructed into either iron girder or reinforced concrete permanent structures. The progress of improvement is higher in percentage than the national average for all.

Meanwhile the number of automobiles within Kanagawa Prefecture has increased by ten times during the 15

years after the last war. And the volume of traffic has increased on the average of 48 percent a year on national highways and 43 percent on other major local highways during the period under review.

It is in the face of such enormous and rapid increase in the volume of traffic that both the Central Government and the Kanagawa Prefectural Government are working together to improve the condition of highways, to meet with the ever expanding requirements, and to speed up such readjustments.

The Kanagawa Prefectural Government at present is working hard to realize its 5-year program (ending 1965) of highway improvement. 100 percent of the national highways are to be improved and newly paved; and improvement work is being carried out on other local major highways, with special attention focussed on their importance in relation to industrial development.

Simultaneously the construction of toll highways is also pushed as part of the national program, according to the plan for completing a national highway network.

Still another greater project is the construction of rapid transit automobile highways connecting Tokyo with Nagoya. The project is still in the survey stage on the proposed two routes of the Central and the Tokaido trunk lines.

In addition, the work has started on the construction of a third highway between Tokyo and Yokohama, in order to mitigate the present overwhelming congestion.

Manazuru toll highway

Shonan Maritime Highway

Yokohama by-pass

Bridges

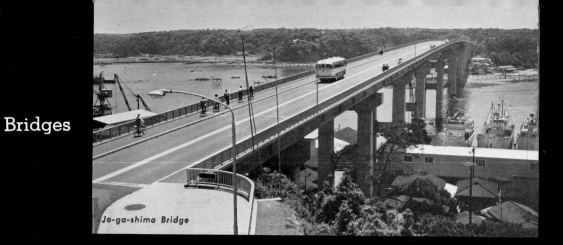

Jo-ga-shima Bridge

Yonegami Bridge

Ranzan Bridge

Haneda Airport — Japan's Front Door

Haneda Airport near Yokohama
(photo : Mainichi Newspapers)

Network of Map of Traffic Kanagawa Prefecture

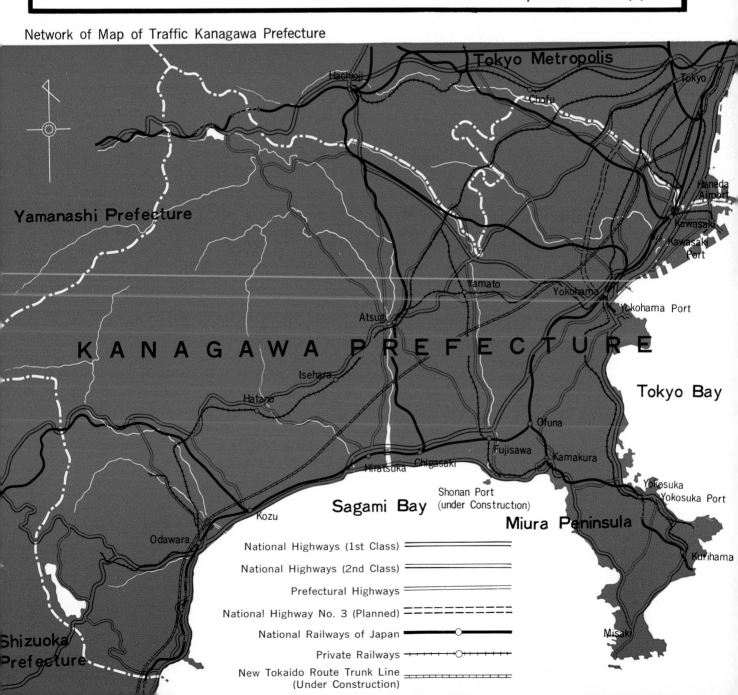

Tokyo Metropolis

Hachioji

Chofu

Tokyo

Haneda Airport

Kawasaki

Kawasaki Port

Yamanashi Prefecture

Yamato

Yokohama

Yokohama Port

Atsugi

K A N A G A W A   P R E F E C T U R E

Isehara

Tokyo Bay

Hatano

Ofuna

Fujisawa

Kamakura

Chigasaki

Hiratsuka

Yokosuka
Yokosuka Port

Shonan Port
(under Construction)

Sagami Bay

Miura Peninsula

Kozu

Kurihama

Odawara

National Highways (1st Class) ═══════

National Highways (2nd Class) ────────

Prefectural Highways ────────

National Highway No. 3 (Planned) ━ ━ ━ ━

National Railways of Japan ━━━○━━━

Private Railways ┼┼┼○┼┼┼

New Tokaido Route Trunk Line ════════
(Under Construction)

Shizuoka
Prefecture

Misaki

Railways

Kanagawa Prefecture may truthfully boast of having a highly developed railway network within its circumscribed area, mainly as a result of its geographical proximity to the capital city of Tokyo, and also because it embraces such important cities as Yokohama and Kawasaki as well as the Keihin (Tokyo-Yokohama) industrial zone.

Along with the endless expansion of these cities, coupled with the spectacular development of industrial activities, both the number of passengers and the volume of freight carried by rail have shown a remarkable increase, particularly in recent years.

During the ten year period from 1950 to 1959, both the National Railways and local private lines recorded increases by two to three times in the number of passengers, and in the volume of freight, from two to four times.

A great congestion is witnessed in the railway passenger service everywhere, particularly during the commutation hours, along the lines directly connecting such established cities as Tokyo, Yokohama and Kawasaki with the suburban residential areas. As the manufacturing industries continue their incessant growth, so the industrial zones also keep expanding, necessitating greater traffic facilities. So much so the railway transportation capacity, in spite of its tremendous improvement in recent years, still falls short of the ever expanding requirements. The inadequacy of the railway accommodations is now held as a bottleneck to further industrial development in this part of Japan.

The National Railways of Japan has worked out a new 5-year program to improve the situation. It has started in the fiscal 1961-62 (ending March, 1962) to deal with the present and future increase in the volume of traffic. Under the new program, construction work is going on in different parts of Kanagawa Prefecture, including the construction of a new, additional Tokaido (Tokyo-Osaka) trunk line.

Local private lines have also taken steps in improving their services, such as increasing the number of railway rolling stock and their modernization, in order to give safer, faster and more pleasant commutation services. They are planning also to build new lines to coordinate their traffic activities with the new city planning programs that are now under way at various places in this Prefecture.

New Tokaido route of the National Railways under construction; limited express trains to run at a speed of 200 km/hr between Tokyo and Osaka.

Limited Express "Kodama"

● Reinforcement
of
Transportation Capacity

Both the National Railways of Japan and private railway companies operating in Kanagawa Prefecture are planning to construct new lines and also to increase the number of trains operated so that their railway transportation capacity will be greatly augmented. Some of the plans have already become actuality.

Among other lines, the National Railways of Japan is already working on the project of a new trunk line along the Tokaido route which is to connect Tokyo with Osaka, to be completed in 1964. The distance between Tokyo and Osaka will then be covered in three hours.

Ports and Harbors

In Kanagawa Prefecture, there are the three major ports of Yokohama, Kawasaki and Yokosuka, and also such local ports as Manazuru, Oiso, Abuzuri and Shonan.

It will be recalled that Yokohama harbor facilities were heavily devastated during the war years, and that the port was taken over entirely by the Occupation Forces during the immediate postwar years. Even at present, the Mizuho Pier and part of the Shinko (New Port) Pier are under the control of the U.S. Security Forces stationed in Japan. Meanwhile the main port of Yokosuka is also under the control of the U.S. Forces at present.

In recent years, however, both Yokohama and Kawasaki play increasingly important role as international trade ports.

The volume of freight exported and imported through Yokohama reached the new postwar high of 22,570,000 tons in 1959 while Kawasaki also recorded a new high of

Volume of Trade Through 3 Major Ports of Kanagawa Prefecture

	Yokohama	Kawasaki	Yokosuka	Total
1947	14			14
	1,641			1,641
1950	485		29	514
	5,128		285	5,413
1955	955	52	6	1,013
	7,639	2,005	172	9,816
1959	1,246	137	24	1,407
	7,637	6,203	205	14,045

☐ Exports   ■ Imports

(Unit: 1,000 ton)

Kawasaki Port

Yokohama Port

18,820,000 tons that year.

Much of harbor improvement work has been carried out in these ports year after year, but such improvement efforts have proved inadequate, in the face of the incessant expansion in the volume of freight traffic, as well as the increase in the number of domestic and foreign ships that visit these ports.

Under the national program of major ports improvement, therefore, Yokohama is going to have four additional quay walls at Yamashita and Hommoku, to be equipped with 36 new berths to accommodate large ocean going liners, in addition to the 36 existing berths; the construction work was started in 1961, to be completed in 1970 when upward of 58,720,000 tons of cargo will be handled through the Yokohama waterfront.

Harbor improvement is also going on at Kawasaki as well, in the face of the recent enormous increase in the volume of cargo traffic at the port's public piers. A feature here is the dredging of the basin in view of the recent trend of an increased size in the type of vessels that visit Kawasaki port.

Meanwhile Yokosuka is not being neglected either; along with the industrial development of the hinterland area, notably Kurihama, harbor improvement is being carried out here also.

As regards the local ports of Manazuru, Oiso and Abuzuri, waterfront facilities improvement has been completed for the present, with an investment of more than ¥400 million since 1948.

The Shonan port is under reconstruction at a budget of ¥1,860 million to be completed in 1964; this port is going to be the yacht harbor in the Olympic Games of 1964, and also a tourist port connecting Enoshima with with the Izu islands.

Yamashita Pier of Yokohama Port being constructed by reclamation

Conservation

There are one hundred rivers in Kanagawa Prefecture including the Tama-gawa, Sagami-gawa and Sakawa-gawa, their combined total length reaching 900 kilometers.

During the war years, uncontrolled felling of trees was carried out in the water resources areas, while the upkeep of river embankments was not well taken care of. Furthermore, new factories were built, and residential areas created along the river valley areas. And the volume of water flowing along these rivers has increased substantially. As a result, flood damage was caused on a number of occasions due to the overflowing of the water into the surrounding area.

As a measure to deal with such a situation, various programs of river conservation have been worked out, and they have been put into practice with telling results.

In 1943, a forestry conservation program was drafted by the Central Government, and important river resources areas were designated by the State as such. Subsequently, conservation has been carried out at focal points.

Later, however, in sequence to the unusual natural calamity worked by typhoons, notably by the Kanogawa typhoon of 1958 and the Ise Bay typhoon of 1959, a general improvement program that covers the entire length of the major rivers from their fountain head to the river mouths have been worked out.

In Kanagawa Prefecture, work for prevention of sand bars in the rivers as well as general river improvement work are being carried on, in accordance with the foregoing national general improvement program.

During the postwar 15 years, the damage suffered by civil engineering facilities within Kanagawa Prefecture amounted to ¥4,100 million in value. Today, however, the damage done prior to 1957 has been restored completely, and later improvement work is making steady progress.

Conservation work at Mt. Soun area for prevention of sand bars →
An improved river

River Development
and
Utilization

There is a river called the Sagami-gawa in Kanagawa Prefecture. This is the most widely utilized of all the rivers in this Prefecture.

The Sagami-gawa originates in Lake Yamanaka which is located at the foot of Mt. Fuji; it flows from north to south to empty into Sagami Bay.

The Kanagawa Prefectural Government, in 1938, started water utility enterprises on the Sagami-gawa to exploit its water resources for agricultural irrigation and for industrial water and waterworks. The work was accomplished in 1949.

Included among these enterprises was the construction of the first multi-purpose dam in Japan; through the manipulation of this Sagami Dam, the river was used to supply approximately one million cubic meters of water to the prefectural and municipal waterworks of Yokohama and Kanagawa for drinking as well as industrial purposes; in addition, the river now supplies 360,000 cubic meters of water to the plateau area of Sagamihara for agricultural irrigation and other purposes.

Furthermore, the two hydro-electric power stations of Sagami and Tsukui, having a combined total capacity of 54,000 kW, are operated with the water obtained from the Sagami-gawa.

Under the river water utility enterprises, an additional dam of Doshi was built on the Sagami-gawa, and the rivers of Sakawa-gawa and Haya-kawa have been industrially developed in order to promote the hydro-electric power industry, under the direct management of the Kanagawa Prefectural Government. The prefectural power enterprises at present generate 94,750 kW of electricity at the Sagami and six other power stations.

The Kanagawa prefectural waterworks have also seen a substantial expansion in scope in recent years. They supplied more than 31 million cubic meters of water a year to eight cities and towns in the Shonan, Sagami and Hakone areas at the close of 1960. Meanwhile the waterworks to furnish factories with their industrial water have also seen a remarkable expansion; during 1961, the daily supply to such cities as Kawasaki, Yokohama and Sagamihara reached approximately 340,000 cubic meters.

With the recent spectacular development of manufacturing industries and the expansion of city areas, however, the Kanagawa Prefectural Government is in an urgent need of developing new water sources. As a result, the Prefectural Government, in conjunction with the municipal governments of Yokohama, Kawasaki and Yokosuka, have worked out a new general development program to utilize still further the water of the Sagami-gawa.

The new plan calls for the construction of the Shiroyama Dam on the Sagami-gawa in order to preserve surplus water during the high water periods, and also to conduct the water of such tributary rivers as the Nakatsugawa and the Kushi-gawa into this reservoir, thereby obtaining a new supply source of approximately 990,000 cubic meters a day. This water is to be distributed for industrial purposes as well as for waterworks.

The Kanagawa Precefectural Government plans also to build additional power stations at Shiroyama and Sagami, on top of the expansion of existing power stations, to obtain all told 582 million KWH of power.

It is estimated, also, that the construction of additional dams will help control the river water in such a manner that the flood damage will be reduced by approximately ¥50 million a year. The new enterprise is to be completed in 1965.

● Waterworks For All Citizens

Waterworks in Kanagawa Prefecture are operated by such city governments as Yokohama, Kawasaki and Yokosuka in addition to the local facilities run by the Prefectural Government. All told, 2,282,931 persons or 73.5 percent of the total population of this Prefecture are furnished with pure water from these facilities.

The maximum daily supply amounts to 963,584 cubic meters. But the consumption is on a steady increase due to the continuous increase of the population as well as the expansion of industrial activities.

Each and all the existing waterworks have worked out their respective plans of enlargement in their supply capacity, many of them being put into effect. When the new Shiroyama Dam is completed, a daily supply of 581,000 cubic meters will become available.

Water distribution center for various waterworks

The Sagami Dam

A cleaning bed

Lake Sagami

● Waterworks for Industrial Purposes

There are three waterworks for industrial use in Yokohama, Kawasaki and Sagamihara, supplying a combined total of 338,000 cubic meters of water a day.

But there has been an abrupt increase in the demand for industrial water in sequence to the general industrial development.

In order to meet with such an enormous requirement, plans are under way to increase the capacity of these industrial waterworks, along with the progress of construction of the Shiroyama Dam. Upon completion, the daily supply capacity will reach 1,460,000 cubic meters.

In Search of New Water Resources

The Kanagawa Prefectural Government, under the joint auspices of the City Governments of Yokohama, Kawasaki, and Yokosuka started the construction of a dam in the upper stream of the river Sagami-gawa in 1961. The work is to be completed in 1964.

A reservoir extending over 2.39 square kilometers is to be created to contain 54,700,000 cubic meters of water, to supply approximately one million tons of water a day, when the dam is completed.

From the new water resources thus to be acquired, approximately 580,000 tons will be utilized for public waterworks and 420,000 tons for industrial waterworks.

Two hydro-electric power stations are also to be established along with the construction of the dam, to have a combined total capacity (maximum) of 300,000 KWH.

(The section marked in black ink in the picture is to be the reservoir.)

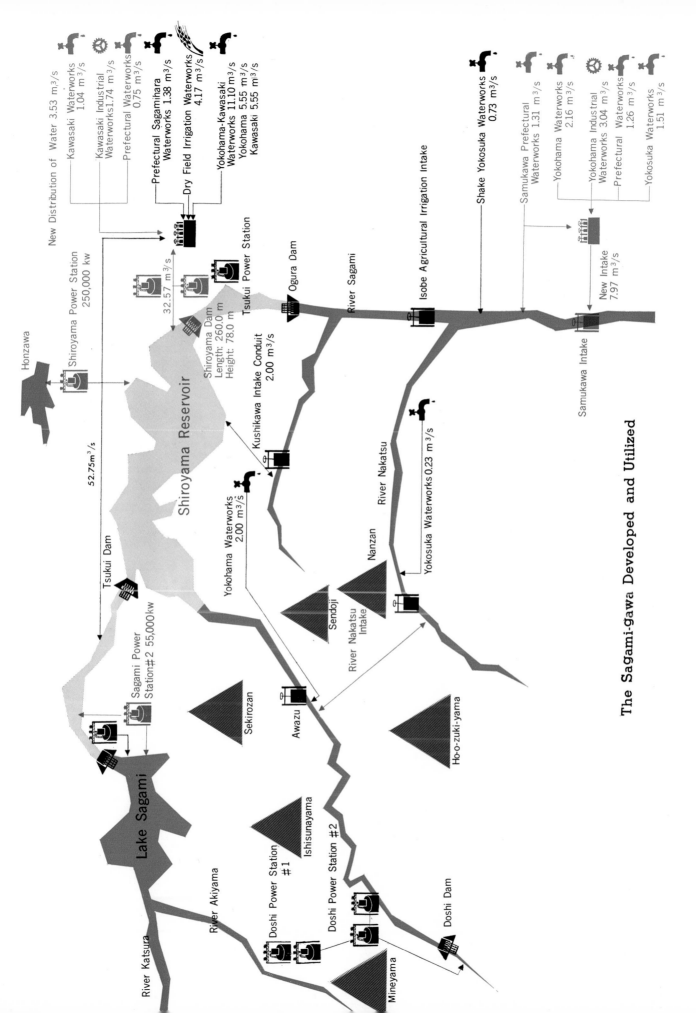

The Sagami-gawa Developed and Utilized

Social Security Buttressed

Social welfare constitutes an important program in the administrative activities of the Kanagawa Prefectural Government. In the postwar years, various systems of social insurance and pension payment, headed by public medical insurance, have been reinforced, along with the inauguration and improvement of various public financial aid systems as well as public and private social welfare enterprises.

The public medical insurance is the nucleus of the social welfare activities; it is put into practice according to two systems: one for working men in regular employment, and the other is for the agricultural and fishing industry populace as well as for the general public not covered by the former system.

The number of persons subscribing to the former system of medical insurance amounts to 660,000; as for the latter, in which the town and village authorities act as the insurer, every resident within the Prefecture has become insured, this measure having been accomplished in 1959. As a result, the number of insured persons has exceeded one million. Their expenses for medical treatment has been reduced substantially.

The national annuity system was inaugurated in 1959 primarily for the purpose of helping those in old age, the physically handicapped, and fatherless families. It has become one of the important pillars supporting social security. In 1959, moreover, aged persons more than 70 years of age began receiving social welfare annuity regardless of whether the individual persons had partici-pated in social insurance or not.

As for the public assistance system, the law for protection of the livelihood of individual persons was enacted in 1950 with a view to giving assurance of minimum sustenance. The number of persons to whom the law is applied within Kanagawa Prefecture has always fluctuated, reflecting the transitional character of social conditions in general; but the number has taken a tendency to decline in and after 1957. As of December, 1960, there were approximately 46,000 persons receiving such public assistance, and the Prefectural appropriations in connection with such assistance exceeds ¥ 2,000 million a year.

In addition to the foregoing, a wide variety of protective measures are in practice, mainly in behalf of the physically handicapped, mentally weak, orphans, the fatherless families, the old aged without supporters, low-income citizens and the like.

It is a fact, however, that much of the favorable effects of social welfare undertakings are attained from private activities of individual social workers and their supporters. There are at present approximately 3,000 persons registered with the Kanagawa Prefectural Government as social workers, such as for public welfare and children's welfare; in addition, there are prefectural, municipal and county councils for local social welfare. All of these organizations and individual social workers together are contributing much toward social welfare in their respective localities.

● Social Welfare Work

Ways and means of social security for the people in their old age have been taken care of to some extent in the form of the establishment of the National Annuity System. Later, however, the establishment of homes for the aged has also been taken up as a national enterprise.

The Kanagawa Prefectural Government, therefore, opened a home for the aged at Kamakura in 1948. In addition, it has inaugurated the system of presenting people in their advanced age with gifts, such as "age respecting money" (as it is called) and memento articles each year.

In behalf of the physically handicapped, the Prefectural Government offers assistance in the way of giving moral and outright financial aid in connection with their livelihood, profession and medical treatment to encourage them to carry on. Moreover, it has opened a vocational training center for the physically handicapped.

As for social welfare measures in behalf of the low-income groups, various local social welfare councils (non-governmental institutions for promotion of social welfare activities) take initiative in offering consultant services regarding their livelihood and professions, and the Prefectural Government gives financial assistance to these institutions in connection with the medical treatment and operating expenses for their program of helping these needy people to be on their own.

A job training facility

A home for the aged

Social Security System 1961

Nomenclature	Object of Insurance		Kind of Payments	No. of Insured within Kanagawa Prefecture (persons)
Health Insurance (By National Govt.) (By Unions)	Laborers in Regular Employment		Payment of Medical Expenses to Insured Persons and Dependents	377,028 214,552
Day Laborers' Health Insurance	Day Laborers		Ditto, above	57,312
National Health Insurance	General Public		Ditto, above	1,017,533
Welfare Annuity Insurance	Laborers in Regular Employment		Old Age, Injury, and Bereaved Family Annuity	755,436
Seamen's Insurance	Seamen		Payment of Medical Expenses and Kinds of Various Annuities to Insured Persons and Dependents	9,625
National Annuity	General Public		Old Age, Injury, Fatherless Family, orphan and Widow Annuity; Payment in Lump Sum at Time of Death	414,545
Accident on Duty Insurance	Laborers in Regular Employment		Medical Expenses and Injury Annuity Pertaining to Accident on Duty	994,246
Unemployment Insurance	Laborers in Regular Employment			807,723

Notes: (1) Not included in this table are various mutual aid systems, pension and retirement allowance annuity system applicable to men in civil service;

(2) Not included in this table are such systems of officially promised aid as the livelihood sustenance law.

For Preservation of Good Health

There has been a marked improvement in Japan's medical institutions as a system. In the 1959 national average, there were 109 practicing physicians, 6.5 hospitals, and 62 general clinics per each 100,000 populace. In the case of Kanagawa Prefecture, the ratio was 145 practicing physicians, 5.5 hospitals and 65.5 clinics per 100,000 prefectural residents.

Generally speaking, however, most of the medical institutions are concentrated in cities. Especially in the prewar years, there was a distinct difference in the distribution of these medical institutions between cities and agrarian areas.

In the face of such a situation, the Kanagawa Prefectural Government made special efforts in the post war years to improve the distribution of medical institutions; it has taken steps to have more hospitals and clinics under the direct management of the Prefectural Government established in the agrarian areas.

Meanwhile there has been a notable development in the progress of medicine as a whole, as well as in the techniques of medical treatment in the postwar years.

Tuberculosis, for instance, used to be at the top of

Transition of Mortality Causes

	1	2	3	4	5	6	7	TOTAL
1959	4,287 21.9% Damage of Cerebral Arteries	2,822 14.4% Cancer	1,910 9.8% Heart Trouble	1,504 7.7% Senility	1,297 6.6% Accidents	1,163 5.9% Pneumonia	937 4.8% Tuberculosis	19,559 (including others)
1954	3,107 16.3% Damage of C.A.	2,267 11.9% Cancer	1,714 9.0% Heart Trouble	1,654 8.6% Senility	1,602 8.4% Tuberculosis	1,135 5.9% Pneumonia	1,024 5.3% Accidents	19,013 (including others)
1949	4,222 18.4% Tuberculosis	2,505 10.9% Damage of C.A.	1,634 7.2% Pneumonia	1,582 6.9% Cancer	1,386 6.1% Senility	1,261 5.4% Heart Trouble	1,086 4.8% Diarrhoea, Enteritis, and Intestinal Ulcer	22,985 (including others)

mortality causes in Japan, and it was at one time described as the "nation destroying sickness", but there has been epochal progress in the method of treatment of this disease, so much so that its ranking in the mortality causes has dropped to seventh.

On the other hand, such adult diseases as heart trouble and high blood pressure have come to the fore among the mortality causes of late, and urgent hope is expressed that something might be done to remedy this new situation.

The Kanagawa Prefectural Government has established the Nagahama Sanatorium to specialize in the treatment of tuberculosis with its modernized facilities. It has also established the Adult Disease Center to combat modern adult diseases.

In the postwar public sanitation administrative activities of the Prefectural Government, the maintenance of good health among the general public has been held as of primary importance. Public hygiene has thus become a matter of first line concern.

In pursuance of the foregoing policy, the Kanagawa Prefectural Government has taken steps in improving sanitation institutions on a wide scope. Among other such institutions, the newly established Odawara Hokenjo is equipped with a hot spring treatment research laboratory, the first in this country. The Prefectural Government thus takes active part in all the programs designed to improve health within the prefecture.

The general public in Kanagawa Prefecture has also come to show much interest and concern about public hygiene.

The poor quality of drinking water in the agrarian districts used to be a problem before the war. In the postwar years, however, local waterworks have been established at various places one after the other. This has materially facilitated the solution of this long pending problem.

The disposal of night-soil and household wastes is now a problem not only in the city areas but also in the countryside as well. The Prefectural Government, therefore, has devoted much time and effort toward the disposal of this sanitation problem. It is also encouraging the establishment of special facilities to take care of the wastes, granting large subsidies to assist with the cost of construction of such facilities.

One of the hospitals in Kanagawa Prefecture

Treatment of tuberculosis

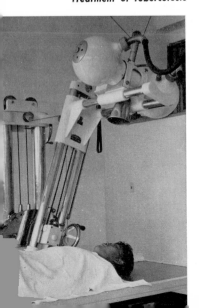

Improvement of Health Centers

Commissioned with the first line duties of safeguarding the public health, the Prefectural Health Centers of Kanagawa undertake the dissemination of information regarding public sanitation, the prevention and combating of epidemics, the improvement of the environment for better sanitation, and hygienic enlightenment campaign for the preservation of good health, particularly of mothers and children.

Since 1951, special efforts have been directed toward the all round improvement and reinforcement of the prefectural health centers, notably to promote programs of combating tuberculosis.

Model health centers have been opened at Hiratsuka and Odawara. In addition, a health center network has been established within Kanagawa Prefecture.

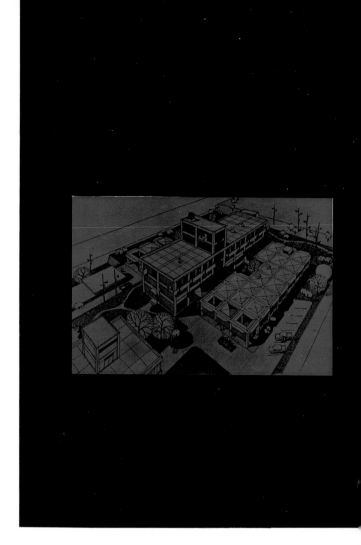

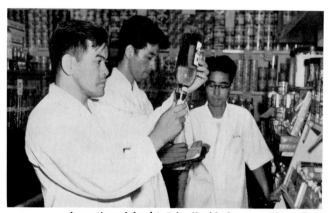

Inspection of foodstuff by Health Center staff members
For prevention of epidemics

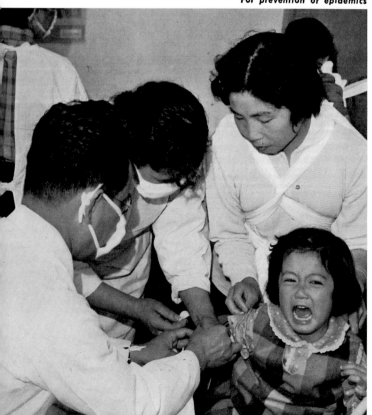

Counter-Measures to Deal With Adult Diseases

In the face of the recent increase in the number of persons who die of such adult diseases as cancer, hypertension and heart trouble, the Kanagawa Prefectural Government is eager to work out counter measures to deal with these mortality causes.

As one of the tangible steps to promote this program, the Kanagawa Prefectural Government in 1961 inaugurated the system of free medical examination for cancer in behalf of the general public resident in this prefecture.

At several prefectural health centers, simple basic physical examinations for early detection of adult disease is carried out for the general public. The Prefectural Government, however, has started building an Adult Disease Center to be completed in 1962, for the purpose of conducting extensive experiments and research as well as giving practical advice for treatment.

76

Progress
in
Physical Culture

The 10th National Athletic Meet, held at various
athletic facilities in Kanagawa Prefecture

Sport events and recreation activities were popularized rapidly and widely throughout the nation in postwar Japan. Many are seen enjoying folk dancing and volley ball not only in the city areas and among employees of various enterprises but also in the countryside as well.

The Kanagawa Prefectural Government has always been eager to promote physical culture among the general public, but availing itself of the opportunity of the 10th Annual National Athletic Meet (which was staged in Kanagawa Prefecture in 1955), the Prefectural Government granted subsidies to have athletic facilities established at different places within the Prefecture, while some of the existing establishments were enlarged.

There are at present 192 athletic facilities, such as grounds for track and field events, baseball grounds, gymnasiums, swimming pools and the like, not including those attached to various schools. Sport events are frequently held at these athletic facilities, but they are also widely utilized by citizens in general as the place of their recreation.

In the forthcoming Tokyo Olympic Games, moreover, the yacht races are to take place at Enoshima and Abuzuri of Hayama, both being within Kanagawa Prefecture. For this purpose, the Kanagawa Prefectural Government has started the construction of Shonan Port at Enoshima, including the construction of a yacht harbor there, in addition to attending to various facilities required for the smooth operation of the races.

● For Coming Olympic Games in Tokyo

Shonan Port construction plan at Enoshima
for the Tokyo Olympic Games of 1964

Working People

As part of economic democratization, the organization of the working classes of men has made a remarkable development in the postwar Japan, along with the national policy to foster labor unions. The manufacturing industries employ the largest number of men and women, and the extent of their organization into labor unions has reached 60 percent.

During the period immediately following the war's end, however, the war devastated industrial zone of the Keihin (Tokyo-Yokohama) area was full of the unemployed, on account of the fact that many people had been repatriated from overseas; the then existing major enterprises had to dismiss employees to reduce the scale of

their industrial activities; and there were many enterprises that had failed.

Japan's labor union movement, in those days, concentrated on labor disputes, notably for wage hikes, and the capital and labor relationships were highly strained.

In 1948, the local labor committee handled 70 cases of labor disputes. Incidentally, social welfare enterprises designed for the alleviation of unemployment began to be carried out at about this time.

Japan's economic situation came to be better stabilized in and after 1951 when business in general began to pick up, leading to a rapid increase in the demand for workers.

There was an all round meteoric development in Japan's

industrial production, but especially remarkable were the enterprises engaged in second-stage fabrication, so much so that the number of workers engaged in this category represented 42.7 percent of the total working populace of Kanagawa Prefecture.

Meanwhile the basic labor law was enacted and promulgated, primarily for the purpose of protecting working people; by virtue of this law, an all round improvement was introduced in the working conditions, e.g., working hours, labor hygiene, safety measures, and special protection of women and juvenile workers.

Such measures as unemployment insurance, casualty insurance, a minimum wage system, and laborers' financial agencies were introduced one after the other for the promotion of working people's welfare. Simultaneously, a mutual retirement allowances reserve system and also assistance in the acquirement of dwelling quarters were introduced, primarily for the improvement of working conditions of people employed in minor enterprises.

The Kanagawa Prefectural Government, ahead of other prefectures, opened the Working Men's Hall in 1949 and the Working Women's Hall in 1954, for the purpose of promoting cultural activities among the working classes, as well as to furnish them with places of recreation. These facilities are in wide utilization by the general public.

The relationships between capital and labor show signs of improvement in recent years, in sequence to the favorable turn of the economic situation in general.

As for employment: there prevails an acute difficulty in acquirement of man power, especially in the employment of younger people graduating from various grades of schools. There is also a marked increase in the demand for skilled labor, reflecting the progress of industrial techniques.

On the other hand, there is much to be done about the employment of those in the middle ages, including those in the employ of the U. S. Security Forces stationed in Japan (where the demand is fast dwindling due to the decrease in the size of the Armed Forces stationed in this country) as well as those who are currently engaged in the enterprises for unemployment relief.

As a measure to deal with this situation, the Kanagawa Prefectural Government follows the policy of reinforcing the facilities of vocational education, thereby to endow unskilled labor with some specialties, incidentally thereby acquiring a larger supply of skilled labor.

Furthermore, efforts are also made to balance the demand and supply of labor mainly through the special activities of such agencies as vocational exchange and the like.

Kanagawa Prefectural Working Men's Hall

Breakdown of Employment : Comparison With National Totals

▓ Primary Industries (Agriculture; Fisheries)
▓ Secondary Industries (Mining; Construction; Manufacturing)
▓ Tertiary Industries (Commerce; Service; etc.)

	Primary	Secondary	Tertiary
Kanagawa Pref.	10%	42.6%	47.4%
National Total	35%	27%	38%

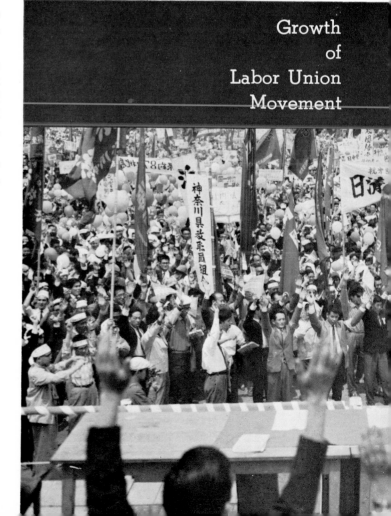

Growth
of
Labor Union
Movement

Fostering of Skilled Labor

A transistor manufacturing factory where everything is neat and clean (photo : Mainichi Newspapers)

There has been an increasing demand for skilled labor in Kanagawa Prefecture in recent years, especially in the heavy industry center of the Keihin (Tokyo-Yokohama) area, in sequence to the remarkable advancement of industrial techniques as well as that in industrial production.

The Prefectural Government has therefore organized vocational training with special emphasis laid on pertinent subjects relating to manufacturing industries in order to bring up skilled labor and technical experts.

There are at present 12 institutions where vocational training is given, the subject taught there including welding, metal plate working, automobile upkeep and so forth, all told numbering 24 in variety. It is scheduled, moreover, that the prefectural vocational training activities will be reinforced on a larger scale.

Working men enjoying recreation at lunch time (an example of employees' welfare facilities)

Training of skilled labor (at a government operated vocational training institute)

For Protection
of
Public Peace

With a view to democratizing the police system in Japan, the decentralization of police power was put into effect in March, 1948; as a result, autonomous police forces of cities, towns and villages were created.

It was then found that the new system was inadequate sometimes, especially in connection with integrated police activities; it was also found that the new system incurred exceedingly heavy burdens upon the finances of local governments.

A wholesale innovation of the new police system was then put into effect in 1954 by virtue of the revision of the police law; subsequently, the present system of having each prefecture as the individual unit has been established. And the Kanagawa Prefectural Police was thus created.

There are at present 38 police stations in Kanagawa Prefecture, with 285 precinct stations constituting the lower structure, and there are 6,287 policemen on the staff.

Besides being one of the active industrial areas in Japan, Kanagawa Prefecture embraces the world famous international trade port of Yokohama. In addition, there are such operation bases of the U.S. Security Forces stationed in Japan as Atsugi, Zama, Yokohama and Yokosuka within the Prefecture.

In view of such a peculiar background, the Kanagawa Prefectural Police have to deal with such offenses as international smuggling, narcotic traffic, and peculiar violations of laws pertaining to pharmaceutical stimulants and the like, in addition to ordinary criminal offenses in general.

In order to cope with such characteristic situations of policing, the Kanagawa Prefectural Police have taken steps toward better organization of the police force, the promotion of scientific techniques of investigation, general improvement of police facilities, rational distribution of the patrol duty policemen and so forth.

On the other hand, the recent enormous expansion of the city limits along with the development of industrial activities, new residential areas and factory zones have been created on a large scale in the hinterland districts. Incidentally, it has given rise to the need of having better fire fighting facilities.

Furthermore, as the mode of living in general has become more complicated as well as more modern, it has also become necessary to introduce qualitative improvement of the fire fighting units in the way of modernization, e.g., the need of having more fire-engines equipped with high-pressure pumps and longer life-saving extension ladders to deal with tall buildings, not to mention fire-engines equipped with facilities for fighting chemical fires.

The Kanagawa Prefectural Government endeavors to popularize fire prevention awareness among the general public, along with their efforts toward having better means of fighting fires.

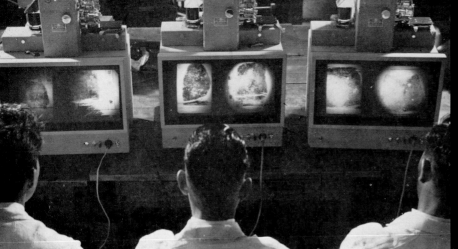

Scientific man-hunt

⬤ For Traffic Safety

In sequence to the recent enormous increase in the volume of automobile traffic, the number of accidents has also been on a steady increase. And it has become one of the most important duties of the Kanagawa Prefectural Police to enforce traffic safety.

The Kanagawa Prefectural Police, consequently, are making serious efforts toward the elevation of the public morality in highway traffic as well as in the propagation of traffic safety ideas, through the means of reinforcement of control of traffic offenses and mobilization of motorcycle patrol officers.

The Bugle Corps of Kanagawa Prefectural Police

Fire Fighting

Modernized fire fighting (life-saving extension ladders, and fire engines equipped with faciiities for fighting chemical fires are utilized)

Fire fighting boat (for fighting fires on water)

He Who Shoulders the Next Generation

Japan's school system was subjected to a fundamental reform in March, 1947, by virtue of the new basic education law; the nine year compulsory education system generally known as the Six-Three System was established, simultaneously with the introduction of co-education.

A qualitative change was also introduced in subject matter taught at schools; the new policy was to attach greater respect to individual personality and also to follow more pragmatic lines of teaching, instead of education centered about the State and family of heretofore.

At the time when the new Six-Three System was put into practice, however, much inconvenience was experienced in connection with school accommodations.

For one thing, many schools were war-devastated, especially in city areas. And the period of compulsory education was increased by one year. There were more students than the existing class-rooms could accommodate.

Schooling in two shifts and that in over-crowded class rooms was a common pratice among primary schools and junior high schools in those days.

Today, however, such an abnormal state of affairs has been remedied, except in limited areas in large cities; more schools have been established with an all round improvement of facilities that go with the new system.

The question at issue in Kanagawa Prefecture today is the need for more school accommodations and facilities for high school education; this is because a larger number of students, who were born immediately after the war during the so-called " baby boom " period, are ready to advance to high schools now.

Another problem is vocational education; in view of the fact that Kanagawa Prefecture embraces the Keihin

Ratio of Advancement to High Schools

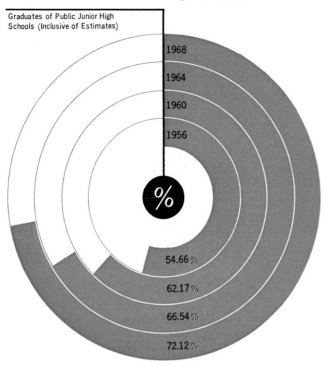

Graduates of Public Junior High Schools (Inclusive of Estimates)

1968
1964
1960
1956

%

54.66 %
62.17 %
66.54 %
72.12 %

(Tokyo-Yokohama) industrial zone, there is an urgent demand for skilled labor.

Up to fiscal 1963-64 (ending March, 1964), the 41 existing high schools are to complete their expansion programs by having additional facilities. In addition, three new high schools and four technical schools of high school standard are to be created during the period under review.

Since the private school law was promulgated in 1949, there has been a remarkable development in this field. There are at present 150 private schools of primary, junior high and high school levels, enrolling 84,541 students. The Prefectural Government grants subsidies to these private primary, junior high and high schools for the improvement of school facilities, independent of what is being done in other prefectures.

There are 11 colleges and universities, including Yokohama National University, Keio University and so on, in addition to 11 more junior colleges. All of these colleges and universities are equipped with fine facilities for the general promotion of learning and education, thereby contributing substantially to the elevation of the education level of Kanagawa Prefecture.

(above) *A primary school compound between lessons* (below) *The entrance ceremony at a university*

Number of Primary and Junior High Schools and Classes

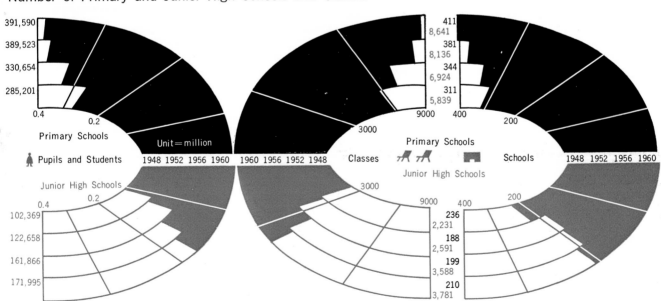

391,590
389,523
330,654
285,201

0.4
0.2

Primary Schools

Pupils and Students
Unit = million
1948 1952 1956 1960

Junior High Schools

0.4   0.2
102,369
122,658
161,866
171,995

411
8,641
381
8,136
344
6,924
311
5,839

9000   400   200

3000

Primary Schools

Classes   Schools

1960 1956 1952 1948

Junior High Schools

1948 1952 1956 1960

3000

9000   400   200

236
2,231
188
2,591
199
3,588
210
3,781

● Special Schools

There are two schools for the blind, four schools for the deaf, and two schools for the physically weak within Kanagawa Prefecture. At these schools for the blind and deaf, special vocational training is also given to enable them to be self-supporting in their adulthood, in addition to general curriculum.

Industrial education

A private school (photo : Keio University)

School Hygiene

In the field of public school hygiene, it will be noted that the school lunch program was inaugurated after the war, as a measure to prevent the deterioration of children's physical welfare, in the face of an acute shortage of food that prevailed throughout the nation at that time.

School children's physical condition was restored in 1951 to the prewar peak of 1939, and aforementioned school lunch program had thus attained its primary objective. Nevertheless, it was then decided that this system should stay in practice, in consideration of the fact that it contributed much toward the attainment of favorable results, in the domain of school education.

During this time, the frequency of tuberculosis among the school children has declined from 1.3 percent in 1951 to about one-quarter thereof. On the other hand, an annual increase is reported of the cases of decayed teeth. As a measure to deal with such a development, the Prefectural Government inaugurated in 1950 the system of school circuit dental inspection, in order to arrest the further progress of such a tendency.

As for physical culture, the policy is to foster the basic ability to perform athletics as a rule.

A circuit dental clinic car

Physical culture for primary school children

For the present, approximately 89 percent of primary school children and 5 percent of junior high school students are provided with food at school.

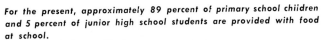

For the Wholesome Growth of Teenagers and Youths

One of the biggest social problems in postwar Japan concerned itself with inappropriate activities of younger folks.

Immediately following the termination of World War II, cases of juvenile delinquency and criminal offense showed a conspicuous tendency to increase, in the face of the social chaos and hardship of living.

Better social order was restored later, and the national life has been more or less stabilized, but the foregoing trend of undesirable activities of youths has remained unabated, so much so that in 1955 the juvenile offenses amounted to 16% percent of the total cases of criminal offenses in general.

The Japanese Government, in concert with prefectural and other local governments as well as non-governmental institutions, has made serious efforts toward the guidance of teenagers and youths to protect them from deviation into undesirable channels. As one of the measures to deal with youth problems, what is called Youth Problems Council was established with prefectures, cities and counties as the constituent units.

The Kanagawa Prefectural Government, in 1960, promulgated regulations designed to foster wholesome growth of younger folks. Furthermore, it has subsidized city, town and village offices to establish local playgrounds and "Juvenile Halls" in order to furnish children with places of recreation. A total of 44 such facilities for children's welfare were newly completed by the end of 1960.

A new hall to function as a Youth Center is now under construction to be completed in 1962.

On the other hand, what is known as the law for promotion of children's welfare have been enacted. As a result, such enterprises as juvenile consultation institutions, special facilities for orphans as well as the mentally weak, and physically handicapped and the like have been established, these organizations playing a big role in offering assistance and guidance to teenagers and youths.

● Organized Activities of Youths

Kanagawa Prefectural Government is interested in and encourages the promotion of youth organizations as well as in their organized activities. By way of materializing the spirit of such a policy, the Prefectural Government has established youth hostels and also athletic facilities. It also exercises much effort toward the bringing up of leaders in such organized youth activities.

The children's societies, spontaneous organizations for children, were promoted after the last war under the able guidance of the prefectural education committee members, primarily for the wholesome development of children's daily activities outside their school.

A commendable growth has been apparent in this project thereafter, as evidenced by the fact there were approximately 3,000 such societies within this prefecture in 1961, participated in by approximately 270,000 children. The number corresponds to 65 percent of the primary school children and 8 percent of the junior high school students in this Prefecture.

Youth Center

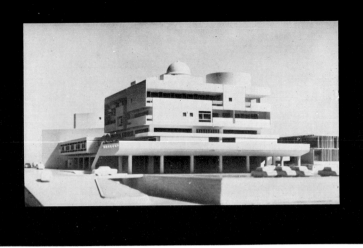

A plan is under way to construct a Youth Center for the purpose of facilitating various activities designed to assist wholesome growth of teenagers and youths.

It will be a four-story building with basement; it is to house therein a theater with a seating capacity of 1,000; a library; a music hall; a planetarium; a scientific experiment room; the United Nations Room; and so forth.

The Youth Center is to be built on Momiji-ga-Oka Hill of Yokohama City, adjoining the Prefectural Library and the Music Hall. The construction will be completed in the fall of 1962.

Children's playground

Young Japan (mountain climbing for recreation)

Juvenile Social Welfare

Japan's law for promotion of children's welfare was promulgated in 1947 to replace the old manner of thinking of protecting specific children who need be protected, with a new positive philosophy of promoting the welfare of all the children who are to shoulder tomorrow's responsibility of the nation. The juvenile consultant institutions have been organized as a result in 1948 to receive consultations, to offer guidance, and to give assistance on all juvenile programs.

In the early stage of their activities, however, these juvenile consultant institutions were busy dealing with war orphans and juvenile delinquents.

It is only in recent years that the general public has come to avail themselves of these institutions in connection with the training of their children and the like, thus the primary objective of these institutions becoming better understood by the public.

During this time, special facilities for the benefit of orphans, the physically weak, physically handicapped, and mentally weak have been established. These institutions not only offer protection to these children but also help them to obtain some vocational training so that they may become able to be on their own in their adulthood.

Numerically largest are the special dormitories for fatherless families and also the public nurseries, and these institutions have played a big role in assisting fatherless families whose number had suddenly increased after the last war.

Nursing home for orphan babies

Learning to walk (the physically handicapped)

Child Consultation Office

Orphans going to school

An institution for the physically handicapped the Yukari (Eucalyptus) Institute

Level of Living Improved

On a picnic in the suburbs

Vacationing at the seashore

At a farm house today (note that the mode of life is about the same as that in the city areas)

The individual income of people in Kanagawa Prefecture has recorded a steady increase as a result of the economic growth and the level of living has also gradually improved.

The per capita income of the people of Kanagawa Prefecture in 1959 amounted to ¥144,300 which represented an increase of 1.8 times, even with a discount for the rise in commodity prices, as compared with that of 1951 or thereabout.

There has been an all round improvement in the people's livelihood; the sales of clothes increased by 2.4 times while such electrical appliances as television sets, electric washing machines and the like are finding their way into individual households in great abundance.

People's savings are also increasing, indicating a surplus in their individual incomes.

On the other hand, recreation activities have become popularized in cities as well as in the countryside, with a result that hot springs and tourist centers are crowded with people who visit them in their leisure.

Greater Interest
in Cultural Life

Freedom of thought and its expression was established in Japan after the last war. Incidentally, it stimulated remarkable cultural activities on all sides, e.g., in literature, theater, music and fine arts, leading to active international cultural intercourse with various nations of the world.

On the other hand, freedom of thought and its expression has also stimulated such cultural activities as "social education" in the form of adult education, along with schooling in general, to play a big role in the promotion of the nation's cultural and intellectual life.

With the better stabilization of the people's livelihood as a back ground, the nation's interest in subjects of fine art and culture was much aroused; and better appreciation of music and fine arts permeated an unprecedentedly wide scope of social strata.

The Kanagawa Prefectural Government has taken special steps in improving cultural facilities for the purpose of augmenting and popularizing social education.

In 1951—or only a few years after the termination of the war—the Prefectural Government established the Modern Art Hall in Kamakura, a city replete with places of historial interest; this enterprise has been carried out in such a scale that it has become one of the most prominent art museums of the nation, so much so that it has attracted a large number of visitors including many foreign tourists.

Furthermore, the Prefectural Government has also established a large concert hall and library in Yokohama, and another library expressedly for industrial and scientific learning in Kawasaki city. At present there are 27 libraries in Kanagawa Prefecture, not including school libraries. These institutions are doubtless playing an important part in the spread of public cultural enlightenment.

A concert hall and a library

Inside a museum
A museum of moderm arts, Kamakura

A circuit library on its tour of agrarian areas

At a library (Kawasaki City)

The Prefectural Music Hall which is known for its excellent acoustics

At a library

Flower arrangement (photo : Mainichi Newspapers)

Tea ceremony

Quite evident in the daily life of the Japanese in general is the fine arts of old Japan with their history and tradition, not only in the form of flower arrangement and tea cult but also in the products of the industrial arts as well as in the everyday household furniture, tableware and the like.

It is a fact that flower arrangement and the tea cult are taught all over the country and that the number of persons who pay tuition for lessons is innumerable. Meanwhile quaint articles of industrial arts and handicraft produced in different parts of the country reflect local color and folklore traditions.

In Kanagawa Prefecture, woodwork of mosaic and inlaid techniques turned out in the Hakone district are specially well known.

96

● Time Honored Customs in Japan

The 15th of November is the day for "Seven, Five, Three" (shichi-go-san) when children who reach the age of three, five or seven some time during the year are taken to a local shrine to pay homage there, dressed in their best kmono or suit.

The Japanese in general are very anxious to start the new year properly, and many a person opens his activity by paying homage at a shrine on New Year's Day. The custom is to buy an arrow at the shrine on the way home, the arrow being a symbol of "shooting troubles" or of scaring "devils" away.

Girls fete the 3rd of March, the Dolls Festival; shown in the picture is the orthodox mode of display of dolls and doll furniture, although

not every home nowadays follows this classical form and style of presentation.

Japan the Beautiful

Japan is known internationally for its scenic beauty and excellent cultural heritage. And Kanagawa Prefecture is one of the representative among various prefectures of Japan specially known for such properties of ancient historical and cultural value, in addition to places of exquisite scenery.

There is Yokohama, Japan's front door for those stepping ashore from abroad; and there is the Fuji-Hakone National Park, not to mention such places of sight-seeing value as Enoshima, Yugawara, and Kamakura, a city replete with relics of historical interest.

The number of foreigners who visit Kanagawa Prefecture has run high since before the last war. The tourist business as such, however, had long remained in a state of complete inactivity on account of the war.

International tourism, however, has been taken up as one of important branches of Japan's postwar national economic policy; efforts have been made for the improvement of facilities catering to foreign tourists, as well as for promotion of publicity with specific end in view of attracting more visitors from abroad.

Presumably in sequence to such intense efforts, the number of foreign tourists visiting Japan has shown a steady increase. In 1959, for instance, foreign tourists visiting Kanagawa Prefecture amounted to approximately 280,000.

The Kanagawa Prefectural Government takes the view that tourism is a major industry, and it devotes special efforts toward the promotion of this enterprise.

Since immediately after the war's end, the Prefectural Government has made large investments in the development of places for international tourism, not only in the establishment of hotel accommodations but also in the all-round improvement of highways, so that foreign tourists may enjoy their visit in comfort.

Kanagawa Prefecture has thus succeeded in the creation of modern facilities for tourism which are indispensable for an easy access to places of scenic beauty and historical interest.

Yokohama

The club house of a golf course

The Sankeien (a landscape garden noted for ancient
buildings collected from varions parts of Japan)

A festival at China Town of Yokohama

Yokohama is Japan's front door. This international port
city has enjoyed prosperity ever since its opening to foreign
trade. There are at present many foreigners living in this
city, and the streets are tinged with an exotic mood.

The so-called bluff area is representative among the
residential quarters of foreigners in Yokohama, together
with the famous China Town and the Foreign Cemetery.

On the other hand, there is Sankei-en which is a typical
landscape garden of Japanese style where the traditional
beauty and characteristic sense of fine art of the nation
are preserved to this day. This garden is noted also for
the presence of various ancient buildings which have been
brought in from various parts of the country.

There are also places of scenic beauty and of historical
interest within Yokohama City, related to Japan's opening
to international associations after the abandonment of the
200 year old seclusion policy.

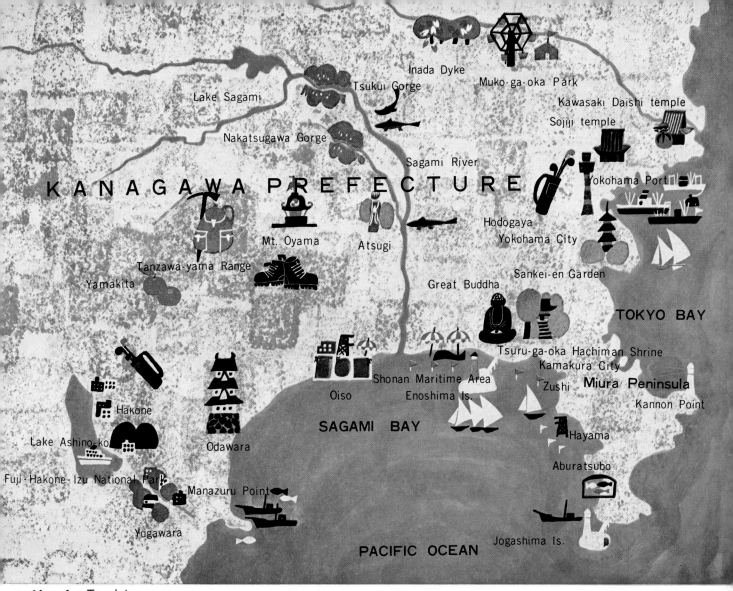

KANAGAWA PREFECTURE

Lake Sagami

Tsukui Gorge

Inada Dyke

Muko-ga-oka Park

Kawasaki Daishi temple

Sojiji temple

Nakatsugawa Gorge

Sagami River

Yokohama Port

Mt. Oyama

Atsugi

Hodogaya

Yokohama City

Tanzawa-yama Range

Yamakita

Great Buddha

Sankei-en Garden

TOKYO BAY

Tsuru-ga-oka Hachiman Shrine

Kamakura City

Shonan Maritime Area

Zushi

Miura Peninsula

Hakone

Oiso

Enoshima Is.

Kannon Point

Lake Ashino-ko

SAGAMI BAY

Odawara

Hayama

Fuji-Hakone-Izu National Park

Aburatsubo

Manazuru Point

Yugawara

Jogashima Is.

PACIFIC OCEAN

Map for Tourists

Tourists stepping ashore at Yokohama

Kamakura, Ancient City of Japan

Together with Kyoto and Nara, Kamakura is a representative ancient city of Japan. The military government of Kamakura, the first of its kind in Japan, was established in this city by the Minamoto Clan some 700 years ago. Kamakura was thus the political and cultural center of Japan for many years thereafter.

Kamakura is replete with cultural heritage, such as shrines, temples and Buddhist statues, much to the pleasure and appreciation of visitors to this city.

The seashore of Kamakura is also famous as a surf bathing site. Each summer, the place is crowded with recreation seekers.

The front gate of the ancient Kencho-ji Temple

The Great Buddha of Hase (Kamakura)

Buddhist priests doing mendicancy as part of their penance

The Hachiman Shrine of Tsuru-ga-Oka (Kamakura)

Enoshima

Surf bathing around the Shonan area

White sand and green pine trees add so much to the picturesque scenery of the Shonan maritime area, especially with Enoshima—an islet covered with trees—seemingly afloat on the sea off the beach to the south of Katase, waterfront of Fujisawa City which is situated in the central part of the Shonan area.

Enoshima is connected with the Main Island by a bridge. But the sea around here is shallow for a great distance, constituting one of the most popular surf bathing areas of the nation.

A spacious area along this seacoast has been made into the Shonan Maritime Park which is dotted by such modern facilities as hotels, rest houses and an aquarium.

There is at present under construction a tourist port on Enoshima, along with a yacht harbor which is already designated as the site of yacht races for the coming Tokyo Olympic Games of 1964.

Shore-fishing

Shonan maritime highway

At Aburatsubo (Miura Peninsula)

Anglers enjoy fishing in a river, especially in fishing season for "ayu" and river trout; many assemble from all parts of the country to exchange "fish stories" over a dinner of their trophies.

106

Hatano basin (tobacco cultivation center)

Hakone

Mt. Hakone is favored with exquisite scenic beauty and many hot springs. Designated as the Fuji-Hakone National Park, the area is one of the most popular resorts for tourists.

Mt. Hakone used to constitute a natural barrier to traffic and communications between the West and East of Japan's Main Island. And there are many places of historical interest from the Kamakura Period (1193-1392) to the Edo Period (1603-1866) as well as a vast cultural heritage.

At present, paved highways run in all directions throughout the mountainous area to afford pleasant drives, while quaint pleasure boats are operated on its lake. Moreover, such modern facilities as hotels of the Western and Japanese styles are established here. Still more recently, rope way and cable car systems have been built to attract visitors throughout the four seasons of the year.

The Kanagawa Prefectural Government has inaugurated the Hakone Tourist Center in the central part of this pleasure resort. In addition, a plan is under way to establish international conference facilities at Hatabiki-yama which is noted for its command of the grand view including Lake Ashi-no-Ko below.

By the shore of Ashi-no-Ko (lake)

(above) *Mt. Hatabiki-yama and vicinity (counted among the sites for the construction of an International Tourist Hall)*

(below) *The Hakone by-pass (built for the alleviation of traffic congestion around the pleasure resort of Hakone)*

● Hostelry

There are 16 hotels within Kanagawa Prefecture which are designated by the Central Government as international tourist hotels. In addition, there are other hotels which are capable of accommodating foreign visitors. Their combined capacity is approximately 6,000 persons.

Meanwhile the construction of new hotels is going on at principal places of tourist interest. It is expected that their capacity will be enlarged substantially within a matter of a few years.

Hakone Tourist Hall (a prefectural institution)

The Owakidani Valley
where the brimstone moutains regurgitate sulpher gases

Suspension cable cars

A hot spring town Yugawara

There are several golf courses at Hakone

(left) Mt, Fuji and Ashi-no-Ko (lake)

● Annual Festival Activities

There are many annual functions of historical interest observed in Kanagawa Prefecture in view of the fact that this Prefecture embraces such ancient places as Hakone, Kamakura and Odawara.

In addition, there are a number of annual events which participated in by foreign residents in Japan, incidentally revealing the fact that Kanagawa Prefecture has long been Japan's contact point with the West.

Kifune-Matsuri is one of the three great boats festivals of Japan.

A sacred dance by the Shrine Maidens of the Afuri Shrine

Known as "yabusame", archery from the back of a horse running at full speed, is one of the time-honored annual events of Kamakura.

The procession of a feudal lord, a quaint performance reproduced to show how Mt. Hakone was traversed in olden times.